Papers Toward A Radical Metaphysics
ALCHEMY

CHARLES PONCÉ

North Atlantic Books, Berkeley, California

Papers Toward A Radical Metaphysics: Alchemy

Copyright 1983 by Charles Ponce

ISBN 0-938190-01-6 (cloth)
ISBN 0-938190-02-4 (pbk.)

Published by North Atlantic Books
2320 Blake Street
Berkeley, California 94704

Cover art and illustrations by Michael Maier, *Atalanta Fugiens*, 1617

Cover and Book Design by Paula Morrison

Typeset in Paladium by Jed Rasula

Papers Toward A Radical Metaphysic: Alchemy is sponsored by the Society for the Study of Native Arts and Sciences, a nonprofit educational corporation whose goals are to develop an ecological and cross-cultural perspective linking various scientific, social, and artistic fields; to nurture a holistic view of arts, sciences, humanities, and healing; and to publish and distribute literature on the relationship of mind, body, and nature.

Library of Congress Cataloging in Publication Data

Poncé, Charles.
  Papers toward a radical metaphysics.

  1. Psychology—Philosophy. 2. Metaphysics.
3. Mythology. 4. Archetype (Psychology) 5. Change.
I. Title.
BF38.P63   1983   128   83-23832
ISBN 0-938190-02-4
ISBN 0-938190-01-6 (pbk.)

CONTENTS

In Praise of Bombast   11

Paracelsus and the Wound   19

Saturn and the Art of Seeing   29

An Alchemical Allegory: Notes Toward an
     Understanding of Genesis   57

Woman, the Feminine, and Alchemy   73

On the Androgyne   91

To My Mother

"Ithaca has given you the beautiful voyage."
Cavafy

ACKNOWLEDGMENTS

"In Praise of Bombast" was a Foreword to the Shambhala Publications Reprint of *The Hermetic and Alchemical Writings of Paracelcus*, in two volumes, (Berkeley, Ca., 1976).

"On the Androgyne" was delivered as a lecture at the *Age of Androgyne Conference* in November 1976 in Chicago.

"Saturn and the Art of Seeing" was delivered as a lecture at the *Astrology and the Helping Professions Conference* in November 1977 in San Francisco. "Paracelsus and the Wound" was delivered as a lecture at the *Astrology and the Healing Arts Conference* in 1979. Both lectures were sponsored by the National Council for Geocosmic Research.

"Woman, the Feminine and Alchemy," and "An Alchemical Allegory" first appeared in *Maitreya* 4 & 5 (1973 & 1974). 'An Alchemical Allegory" also appeared in revised form in *Arche: Notes and Papers on Archaic Studies* (1978). All pieces have been revised for this publication.

"Human life is in danger right from the beginning: it is promised neither on an archetypal nor a biological plane. It must come into being of its own material and make its psyche and spirit out of itself, its body. No matter how many transcendental planes there may (or may not) be, we cannot overlook or escape the sheer immensity of creation on a purely physical plane. The alchemists who sought to raise spirit or soul ever out of matter, uncommon substance out of common, and gods themselves out of ashes, understood implicitly that we are bound by our mortality. The decay and pain around us is not the wasting and grief of a mere residual world in which we chanced to occur; it is the decay and pain of us, the fact of our substance. We put on the mortal coil with great difficulty and minute precision; we cannot be abstracted from it, and we cannot idealize our wholeness and mentation as if it were solely angelic or metaphysical. The crisis of our becoming is real, not the image of a higher dimensional realm and not the symbol for another mortality."

—from *Embryogenesis* by Richard Grossinger

PREFACE

The papers that follow were created over a period of ten years either in the form of articles, lectures or introductions to other works. Each of them deals with issues and images central to traditional alchemical concerns. Some approach alchemy from a psychological perspective, others from a mythological, and yet others from a metaphysical. That is, three dialects or voices are employed, each nonetheless of the same language.

None to my way of thinking describes what the new metaphysic might be. Some might hopefully point in a general direction, while others point back in time. I would have liked to have been able to tell you what the new metaphysic might be, but all that I can imagine is that we flounder at the tail end of an aeon whose metaphysic sinks into itself. Mircea Eliade once noted that the speed with which humanity presently attempts to discover its origins might be likened to the old folk-belief that the whole of a person's life flashes before their eyes as they die. Some might find it fanciful to liken civilization to a person—body stretched out through the centuries, history its life, this moment the time of its dying. But there is a certain amount of truth to this image. The historical person is the aeon, the millennium that quickly draws to a close before our eyes. This time dies and all of our modern fears regarding the possibility of the planet's destruction are essentially deep intimations of a death occuring at the collective perimeter of our souls.

History appears to inform us that apocalyptic fears arise at times of great transition. Every such change is at first experienced as a death unless there is available a metaphysic that sees in such endings images of regeneration and rebirth. No such metaphysic appears to be presently available. But alchemy, that metaphysic shelved with the advent of science, the art which strove to transform endings into births (which itself was put to an untimely death because of a misunderstanding) might give us a clue.

It is with such hope that these imaginings are offered.

IN PRAISE OF BOMBAST

"Let him not be another's who can be his own."
Paracelsus

The hard facts concerning the man are as follows: he was born on the shore of Lake Zurich on November 10, 1493 as Philippus Aureolus Theophrastus Bombastus von Hohenheim and was interred in the cemetery of St. Sebastian in Salzburg on September 21, 1541 as Theophrastus Paracelsus. His physician father, Wilhelm von Hohenheim, the bastard son of Georg Bombast of Hohenheim near Stuttgart, Grand Master of the Order of the Knights of St. John, journeyed penniless to Switzerland and settled in the old canton of Schwyz. There, in an inn close by the Devil's Bridge, he met and married Elsa Ochsner, the inn-keeper's daughter who served as a nurse's aid at a nearby hospital. Subject to manic depressive states, she was to leap from the Devil's Bridge into the Siehl River nine years after the birth of Paracelsus. Father and son left shortly afterwards for the outpost of the German Empire, Villach, where Wilhelm became an instructor at a school of mining. It was here where Paracelsus, working as an assistant to his father, first came into contact with alchemy before setting out into the world at the age of fourteen to become the phenomenon that he intrinsically was.

History tells us that the grown Paracelsus was a difficult man, prone to outbursts of invective aimed at the established medical and spiritual authorities of his time. He abhorred untested theory and kicked against the one-sided metaphysical views of his peers with the equally one-sided and abrasive certainty of his experience. During his brief and ill-fated position as Professor at Basle, he invited to his lectures barber-surgeons, alchemists, apothecaries, and others lacking academic background as an expression of his belief that only those who actively practised an art knew it. "The patients are your textbook," he pontificated, "the sickbed is your study," heaping abuse upon the heads of medical students who never saw a patient before their graduation. He ridiculed those who placed more importance on titles than practice and solemnly declared that "if disease put us to the test, all our splendor, title, ring, and name will be as much help as a horse's tail." He was the first to ever lecture in the language of the street, rather than in the official academician's Latin, and the first publicly to condemn the medical authority of Avicenna and Galen, flinging their writings into a bonfire on St. John's day in 1527. As for the renowned Celsus, whose medical theories held sway at the time, he declared that he was (and it was true) better and beyond Celsus—*para-celsus*—. He was run out of Basle.

The conviction of his own experience and practice eventually paid off: he invented chemical urinalysis, chemical therapy, and suggested a biochemical theory of digestion. He demanded that the application of cow dung, feathers, urine and other obnoxious concoctions to wounds be given up in favor of keeping the wounds clean, stating, "If you prevent infection, Nature will heal the wound all by herself." Thus, he anticipated modern techniques of antiseptics by several centuries. In a posthumous treatise on syphilis containing the most comprehensive clinical description the period ever produced, we find that he was the first to perceive that the disease could only be contracted by contact. He was the discoverer of the mercury treatment for the disease as well. Germ theory was anticipated by him in his proposal that diseases were entities in themselves, rather than states of being, that invaded the body to fight with the *archeus* (vital or spiritual force). He therefore gave birth to clinical diagnosis and the administration of highly specific medicines rather than the traditional cure-all remedies of the time. Out of this there also arose the important issue of properly measured dosages for specific ailments. He called for the humane treatment of the mentally ill (but was again ignored for several centuries), seeing in them not creatures possessed by evil spirits but "brothers" ensnared in a treatable malady. Refuting the traditional claim that mental illness was a sin in need of exorcism, he called for a medical approach that concentrated on the treatment of spirit rather than the punishment of body.

He introduced the black hellebore to European pharmacology, prescribing the correct dosage necessary to alleviate certain forms of arteriosclerosis, and recommended the use of iron for "poor blood," emphasizing the importance of employing only the product of plants and not metals. To all of this we can also credit Paracelsus with the creation of the terms "chemistry," "gas," and "alcohol" as well as the discovery of zinc as the active ingredient in the production of brass. And, yes, we can also credit the thrones of his personality for the traditional belief that the word "bombast" was forged by others out of his family name in memory of his irrascibility.

And all of this, along with his numerous writings on practically every area of medical concern (enough to fill two thousand six hundred folio pages of the 1616 edition of his works) was accomplished against the backdrop of an itinerary that would exhaust the most accomplished of modern-day jet-setters: France, Germany, Italy, Denmark, the Netherlands, Sweden, Russia, Spain, England, the Holy Land, Alexandria, the Balkan peninsula, Cyprus, Rhodes, and (as some of his writings appear to indicate) Kos, Samos, and Lesbos. Everywhere he set foot he sought the practitioners of his art at levels of society foreign to the academic world. In time he would become the most accomplished of physicians on the Continent, the lover of the impersonal in humanity: it was the illness in his patients which drew out the vast store of warmth and eros he reserved solely for them. So much for the facts surrounding the human called Paracelsus.

* * *

Up until the appearance of the storm called Paracelsus, alchemy and medicine employed the traditional theories of the philosopher Aristotle and the physician Galen. Aristotle's four element theory remains with us today in Astrology, so we need not review its principles here. Besides, it was with Galen that Paracelsus took issue.

Galen had appended to the Aristotelian theory of the elements the Hippocratic doctrine of the four humours believed to be contained within every body: the blood, the phlegm, the yellow bile, and the black bile. These gave rise respectively to the four tempers: the sanguine, phlegmatic, choleric, and the melancholic.

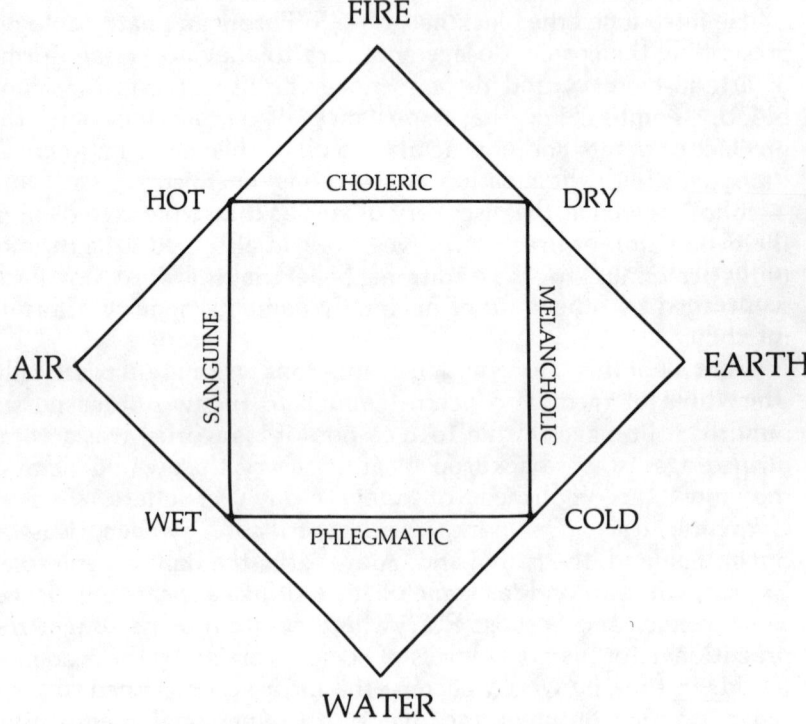

Centuries later the great Arabic alchemist, Jabir ibn Hayyan, further modified the Aristotelian thesis. Whereas Aristotle stated that minerals and fusible metals came into being through the activity of two different smoky and vaporous exhalations, Jabir stated that the two exhalations actually created an intermediary stage governed by Sulphur and Mercury. He held that it was the combination of these two substances in varying degrees that gave rise to metals and minerals. The whole of Western alchemy thereby became grounded in Jabir's theory, until Paracelsus came along.

Jabir's amendments to the Aristotelian element theory did not in any way affect its use in medicine. The Galenic thesis reigned supreme and the introduction of Jabir's emendations served to do nothing more than separate the issue of soul and body. The body was under the reign of the four humours and they in turn were governed by the planets; the soul of the elements, and therefore of the universe, became the concern of the alchemists. True, the planets figured in alchemy, but only in regard to psychic or spiritual realities, not the realities of physical ailments. The Galenic doctors operated under the principle that "contrary cures contrary," and thus administered "dry" remedies for "moist" diseases, cold for hot. These remedies or "Galenicals" as they were called, were primarily created out of herbal concoctions. Obviously, from what we know today concerning the curative power of herbs, they were on to something. Yet, as far as Paracelsus was concerned they were fools and charlatans for they knew nothing of chemical and mineral therapy.

The first thing he did to revolutionize not only medicine but the whole of alchemy as well was to reject the four humour theory and substitute a chemical theory of humours as properties: bitter, sour, salt, and sweet. The body, he insisted, was a chemical system composed of the two alchemical principles sulphur and mercury, to which he added a third principle, salt. In such a manner did the *Tria prima* theory of alchemy appear. Illness arose because of a weakening of the body's defenses brought about by an imbalance of these three principles, thus inviting the *Archei* of disease to invade. The only way to correct this imbalance, Paracelsus insisted, was through the administration of mineral medicines and not the Galenic organic remedies. Thus Paracelsus' entire concern with alchemy was *medicinal* and was quickly to give rise to a branch of alchemists known as iatrochemists—those who solely concerned themselves with the creation of medicines. The rise of iatrochemistry, and of pharmaceutics in general during the seventeenth century, grew directly out of his medical involvement with the theories of alchemy. With one stroke Paracelsus revolutionized centuries of alchemical thought. The difficulties most modern readers have in understanding alchemical texts grows out of this very clear division in the history of alchemical theory. One should ask, with every text published after the sixteenth century, whether or not the basic philosophic stance of the author is Classical or Paracelsian. Then one may safely proceed to other confusing matters.

We therefore have in Paracelsus the reworking of medieval alchemical theory that gave birth to the chemical treatment of physical illness. The man who wrought this change would in time turn to the alchemists from whom he had learned so much and cry, "Don't make gold, make medicines!"

*   *   *

The concept of *daemons*, of guiding spirits or voices couched deep within one's heart or mind, is on the whole preposterous to the twentieth century Western intellect. Rather it is easier to believe in the ability to levitate or teleport than to be victim of an interior guiding spirit. But the Greeks knew and respected this type of experience, as did several of the European alchemists. It is a simple phenomenon, we are told, to which one is inherently susceptible from birth, or which can be laboriously induced through religious or philosophic regime. Paracelsus appears to have been in the class of Socrates — born with the blessing, even driven by it beyond himself. One so possessed tends to trample on convention and convictions, rarely looking back to make excuses. What dictates is a spirited passion for understanding, whose back could be broken by the dialect of what passes for reason, intellectual pomp, and the fear of ostracism by one's fellow persons. Wherever Paracelsus discovered the rigidity of the learned holding sway over the fluidity of the soul, he revolted. His impatience with the vapidness of theoreticians time and again caused him the loss of all social standing and scholarly reputation. One wonders, would these gifts of society have fed the fire of his spirit or quenched it? Such questions call to mind the refusal of the learned to gaze through the devil telescope of Galileo, the terror of Copernicus that he would be discovered as having realized a new theory of the universe, the pitiful figure of Spinoza stretched out in penance before the synagogue, his peers trampling both his spirit and convictions. Better to stand up. In the West, tradition is a great Iron Maiden within which one becomes imprisoned at the first sign of argument. Only a Mercurial Fool like Paracelsus knows how to slip through such spikes of indignation.

We have before us in the man called Paracelsus a human become symbol, an intrusion of archetypal powers onto the human stage; a benevolent possession. When such events occur in the life of an individual, it becomes almost impossible to concentrate on merely one facet of their effect on the world. First and foremost, Paracelsus was a physician. Upon closer inspection he was also a magician, psychologist, astrologer, diviner, pharmacist, philosopher, metaphysician, teacher, reformer, and alchemist. Such a personage invariably attracts the spiritual needs of the generation that looks at him. For one generation he will be the Faustian archetypal quack, another the physician, and for ours obviously the alchemist. There is no way of knowing what he will be called three hundred years from now, what facet of his mind will be pertinent for the spirit of the future. For a little over the past one hundred years it is the figure of the alchemist that has called to us. With every reprint or reconsideration of this thinker and imaginer a different issue in alchemy becomes prominent. I would suggest it is the issue of Imagination more than any other that now presses itself upon us.

At a time when the Western world suffers from an impoverishment of Images, visual representations of modalities capable of exciting a soul battered by the inanities of pure empiricism, there appear again now texts emphasizing the phantastic, the supernatural, the Divine, and all that may be called the Imaginal. It is time we return to the source of our spiritual Imagination so that we may again individually discover the Gods and the powers we vainly attempt to have given to us like frail wafers. The degree to which we have lost sight of our own interiority, our innate ability to introspect, may be best understood when we consider that we must now receive instruction from foreign emissaries of the Spirit in humanity. What is natural in psyche has in our culture become unique, occult, and mysterious. After centuries of denying the Soul its expression, the Spirit its manifestation, we become students again. Paracelsus would have spit in our notebooks.

Alchemy was, and may again become, the archetypal language of the soul. It was the receptacle into which many could deposit the seeds of their peculiar imaginal visions of things to come. It is for this reason that we continually trace so many sciences—chemistry, pharmaceutics, psychology, medicine, etc.—back to it. Alchemy was all of these things and none of these things. It was the product of the Soul Imagining. Paracelsus was no doubt aware of this when he wrote "The power of the imagination is a great factor in medicine." He as few others since allowed the full play of Imagination in the vessel of the art called Medicine.

So, Ladies and Gentlemen, I reinvoke the Imaginal writings of Paracelsus, Lover of Illness. May he guide you to your own souls and their spiritual Health. But take care, for he may spatter your gowns in the process.

PARACELSUS AND THE WOUND

"No one needs to care for the course of Saturn: it neither shortens nor lengthens the life of anybody. If Mars is ferocious, it does not follow that Nero was his child; and although Mars and Nero may both have had the same qualities they did not take them from each other. It is an old saying that 'a wise man may rule the stars,' and I believe in that saying — not in the sense in which you take it, but in my own. The stars force nothing into us that we are not willing to take; they incline us to nothing which we do not desire. They are free for themselves, and we are free for ourselves. You believe that one man is more successful in the acquirement of knowledge, another one in the acquisition of power; one obtains riches more easily, and another one fame; and you think that this is caused by the stars; but I believe the cause to be that one man is more apt than another to acquire and to hold certain things, and that this aptitude comes from the spirit. It is absurd to believe that the stars can make a man. Whatever the stars can do we can do ourselves, because the wisdom which we obtain from God overpowers the heaven and rules the stars."[1]

These are the words of the alchemist and physician Paracelsus who believed that only the doctor who fully understood the heavens could heal the ills of both the body and the mind.

In this paper I would have liked to, had planned to, offer you a litany for the subtle body, a sermon on the importance of your seeing through the ego-bound astrology of the modern world, caught up in the illusion that it is indeed working with the soul. I would have begun by informing you that Paracelsus wrote that ". . . there remains yet another astrology born of the imagination of man, superior to all the rest."[2] In other words, it is not the astrology of the visible world one must pay mind to, but rather the astrology of the invisible or subtle world where powers reside that too many of us have either forgotten or fail to give credence to. I would have begun this work of reclamation by telling you that Paracelsus believed the stars above us could have absolutely no effect upon the stars contained within us unless an intermediary realm—what he called "the star in persons"—was brought into full play. He had written, "Imagination is the star in man," and from this statement I would have much preferred at my leisure to have you understand that Paracelsus meant whatever has appearance also has non-appearance—the subtle, the invisible, and the unseen; that Paracelsus' view was quite explicit: for everything, there is an underthing, the hidden other that makes the thing a dynamic principle; that in his understanding it is not the movement of the planets that affects us, but rather the essence which is contained in the star of imagination, something you cannot chart with an ephemeris. And I would have concluded with his idea that what we too often discover in the synchronistic moment—the moment in which chance has meaning—is nothing more than the outcome of a short-sighted and limited vision of an imagination without depth, one that fails to see beyond such synchronicities to the heart of an imaginal world without end. And I would have finally punctuated his perception that what one should seek with the aid of astrology is not the meaning behind events—for meaning is a human construct, something we create in our attempts to sort our lives out, to find comfort in the manageable and the reasonable—

but rather the power *in* things which is in itself without meaning.

My final paragraphs would have punctuated that for Paracelsus astrology was a tool employed to tell us not only who and what we are, but that we are — that we should look not continually ahead of ourselves to discover when things will be all right (when I will find the right job, when I will be cured, when I will fall in love, etc.) but that things are right as they appear in each moment and that what the moment brings is right. The task of astrology, as that of any helping or healing profession, is to teach us how to carry each moment elegantly, with dignity, for it is the manner in which we receive ourselves that determines whether we grieve or sing, whether what we hear in ourselves is a cacaphony or a melody, whether in that moment we stumble or we dance. That would have been my final statement, but now I will use it as my starting point, having up to this juncture employed as my front man the genius of Paracelsus to which we still aspire centuries later.

Even as I imagined this paper, its focus shifted because of a realization that while much in modern culture concerns itself with the problem of healing, little attention is given to the image of the wound as a physical reality. Our Western concern with health has tended to become an almost spiritual and fashionable affair. The vehicle of this spiritualization has become our new myth, psychology. What I experience in our countless conferences, workshops, and books on health is a new Evangelic Christianization, an aestheticism of disease that all too often equates healthiness with good psychology, soul with some psychological thing called psyche, almost never addressing itself to the body as the carrier of this precious thing. In this regard we must again listen closely to the alchemist Paracelsus:

"The power of sight does not come from the eye, the power to hear does not come from the ear, nor the power to feel from the nerves; but it is the spirit . . . that sees through the eye, and hears with the ear, and feels by means of the nerves. Wisdom and reason and thought are not contained in the brain, but they belong to the invisible and universal spirit which feels through the heart and thinks by means of the brain. All these powers are contained in the invisible universe, and become manifest through material organs, and the material organs are their representatives, and modify their mode of manifestation according to their material construction, because a perfect manifestation of power can only take place in a perfectly constructed organ, and if the organ is faulty, the manifestation will be imperfect, but not the original power defective."[3] In other words, without the proper attention to the body, neither spirit nor soul can impress nor express themselves upon or through us. Thus, we must seriously concern ourselves with the wound. Rarely do we moderns, and one would expect most ancients, turn to ourselves unless we are ill. Few of us pay attention to the interior happenings of our souls, the workings of our bodies, unless something is not working the right way. What brings me to the psychiatrist or internist's office is the wound. It is by the wound that I eventually arrive at a new awareness of something occuring within me. But attending to the wound, I attend to portions of my body and soul that I have ignored. By attending to the wound, I am directed to the particular. My perception of myself as a wholeness breaks down as I now seek to find my wholeness in the wound itself.

This idea is expressed by Carl Jung in his statement that the gods come to us in our diseases,[4] which tells us that in each wound there is a god or a goddess waiting to be discovered, demanding attention. It appears that we now propitiate the gods through our bodies, for they will be propitiated in one way or another. Our bodies have become sacrificial altars. If I am not willing to experience the deity as it is, as a living reality, then it will force me to experience it in my illness, my body becoming a plane of experience for the archetypal.

But there is a general reluctance to accept this idea: people tend naturally to shy away from that which pains. If you ask a person to reflect on a pain or a wound, their immediate reaction is one either of fear or repugnance. The imagery of the wound is sometimes far more real than the wound. A wound can be either ignored or covered over, but few could see it as a mode of transformation. Thus Jung could write that a "neurosis is by no means a merely negative thing, it is also something positive. . . The neurosis contains the patient's psyche, or at least an essential part of it. . . To lose a neurosis is to find oneself without an object: life loses its point and hence its meaning. This would not be a cure, it would be a regular amputation."[5] Here is a good place to remind you that the root of the word cure was "to care," and that our curing today, in the twentieth century, tends to think only of getting rid of. If, indeed, as Jung suggests, the gods now come to us in our diseases, to cure ourselves in this manner would be to rid ourselves of the gods and goddesses. Thus, it is not enough to treat the wound, tend to the disease, with the intent of ridding ourselves of it. We should instead approach each wound, each illness, as a soul-message, an indication that there is something in ourselves we have refused.

Several recent and popular publications have stressed the belief that we should rid ourselves of the morbidity in disease, assume that the metaphors of illness are something that we have imposed upon our bodies, that to be healthy one must in some mysterious manner be freed from the image of illness. The implication is that if illness could be relieved of the metaphors of illness, of the running sore, the cancerous hole in the lung, the crippled spine, that death would somehow become a glorious experience, that we would see life in a new way. But what of the reality of the stinking wound, the stench of terminal cancer? Are we to deny that this is indeed what happens to the body? How can we escape from this reality?

The refusal to see in illness the dark side, the death side, is ultimately a refusal of the gods. And what exactly is so difficult in allowing that what we have or have not done with our souls in some mysterious fashion does indeed bring us into the presence of the god in our disease? What is the cause of this fear of the dark thing in our body and our psyche? How can we expect to realize the whole of life if we do not accept the life we have received *as a wholeness*?

This consequence is in certain ways expressed in mythological and religious symbolism. The wounded god invariably points toward transformation. The imitation of the Christ is finally an imitation of his wounding, of his experience of transformation through the suffering and pain brought about by the conflict of the opposites within us, the suspension of our lives between the two extreme poles of whatever heaven and earth might symbolize for each of us, where we all sooner or later become nailed, fixed, and suspended. It is neither on earth nor in heaven where we suffer our transformation, but somewhere between the two, in a space none of us would consciously create for ourselves, but that nonetheless is a point of embarcation. We tend to overlook the fact that the term synchronicity refers us to accidents—not just any kind of accident, but what Jung called meaningful coincidences in which inner and outer realities suddenly mesh. The message is contained in the accident, and can therefore be an enlightenment of the most painful sort. A synchronicity is the outcome of two worlds clashing to form a bridge for our perceptions. Thus the image of the suspended Christ is a wounding and an accident of the first order, for it did not merely light up the suffering of the god-man on the cross but has lit up the minds and imaginations of millions over the centuries. It was an accident that occurred in the collective psyche, a synchronicity whose effects have still not yet been fully assimilated. Nor should we forget the symbolism of the exiled and wandering Jew, for, as we have each experienced, the wound and the illness exile us from others, drive us into a state of anxious wondering and wandering. Illness removes us from others initially, in some extreme cases separates us from them forever as in the case of the badly deformed or the perpetually infectious. The wound drives us into ourselves, and it is this that allows us an immediate and intimate contact with our souls — if we are capable of receiving it as a numinous event, an archetypal moment that seeks to make us participants in an eternal happening.

I call your attention to the two major images given us by the East and the West: those of the Christ and the Buddha. The Buddha is portrayed in a meditative posture, seated, eyes closed, to all appearances oblivious to the world, unmoved and detached. The Christ on the other hand is painfully alert, almost too much so. These images represent two distinct demands of the psyche upon two distinctively unique cultures. The Buddha, in a culture where pain and suffering, death and disfiguration are an everyday reality (to be seen on almost every street corner) is a symbol of transcendence. By him the Easterner is allowed to discover meaning in an all too painful reality, as well as a way to unite the polarities of suffering and non-suffering through transcendence, through a closing-off of the wound's seepage. The Buddha compensates for collective suffering. But in the West, where consciousness has been focused for so long on controlling nature rather than being in it, we find the compensatory figure of the suffering and wounded person. Thus, the soul of a culture encompasses suffering as a way of transformation. And here I do not mean to suggest that we should move through the world with the vision of a masochist, finding in everything a monster of pure delight, but rather that we do not seek to abolish a certain aspect of nature that cannot be denied.

We rebel against an autonomous principle when we find in disease only a just retribution for our sins or divorce illness and suffering from their own stink—hiding the dying away in sanitary resthomes, refusing to speak about pain and illness at cocktail parties, experiencing a sense of failure when we give birth to the retarded, the crippled, the psychotic—we rebel essentially against the autonomy of Nature, the natural breakdown of Nature, the need of Nature to relax into itself, even to collapse into itself in the way that trees retreat into themselves with the advent of Winter. The proof that we retreat from ourselves, from even our bodies, is to be found in the fact that we in the West must today be taught about the process of dying. We have people come to us, professionals, who actually have to tell us that it is all right to die, that dying is a part of a process, and that it is natural.

And in the midst of all this training something even more disastrous is taking place: an unwillingness to accept the possibility that death is final. We never ask ourselves why we fear our endings, why we create psychological and religious eschatologies that assure us of our continuance. We not only fear endings in relationships, jobs, family, but also the ending of the body. And it is this fear of finality that has contributed to a myth in medicine and the healing arts which (when exaggerated) tortures the dying by refusing to let them die. There is in the twentieth century a denial of death, and this denial is blatantly apparent in our demand that we must rid ourselves of that which is sometimes autonomous in Nature—the wound, illness, and death as finality.

Let me turn this notion on its side, open it a bit more for a closer inspection: I am not denying the possibility that there is a continuance of personality after death, but rather exposing that the recent insistence upon the existence of an after-life, an insistence that is not religious in tone but medical and holistic, is only offered as a reason why we should not fear death. I agree that death should not be feared, and that we should be instructed in the reality of death as process. But I find that in all of this insistence on an after-life the body becomes lost. What we focus on is the soul, or the spirit, or the subtle body in the midst of our death, always turning away from what is immediately occuring. We turn away from our bodies in illness and death not because we have resolved the issue of the wound, but because it is far easier to think of an afterlife, far less fearful and painful to surround ourselves with the good feeling that we may not only escape this life in one psychic piece, but that we will no longer have to concern ourselves with our physical humanity.

This approach to death robs us of our tie to Nature, strips us of our humanity in favor of an exquisite angelology of ego. It allows us to slip past the experience of a mystery: that the body is indeed a great temple which moves slowly towards a breakdown and dissolution. The alchemists knew this: that the soul cannot fly, cannot be released from its vessel until the body is broken down, dissolved, and even putrified. When you read the alchemists you will discover that this breakdown and dissolution is the beginning of the Great Work, and that without experiencing and seeing, watching and attending to this momentous operation—keeping the fire of heart and attention at the proper degree—nothing happens. The soul does not fly, the subtle body is not created, nor is the imagination which is the soul's experience of itself opened into eternity. It is this focus on the body and the wound in both life and death that leads to the sacred marriage of the alchemists. Paracelsus stressed, "The eternal is a sign of the dissolution of Nature, and not the beginning of created things, and the end in all things which no nature is without."[6]

In closing I would like to suggest that astrology not simply focus on healing us of life, of moving us away from body into the eternal, secure in our release, but that it remind us that the four elements of astrology referred to the body and not only the mind; that it is not the soul alone which must be healed, but rather as Paracelsus put it, the organs, through which the soul expresses itself. A true medicine and counselling should therefore be one that addresses the immediate, the body of things and the body, for if we really wish to enter into the eternal, see the universe in a grain of sand, we must in our imagination understand that the horoscope is the soul's expression of itself through body, and that woundedness, disease, and the *putrefactio* of our humanity are for us in the West ordained as the focus of a yoga that sees in these sufferings the gods we have rejected.

NOTES

[1] quoted in *Paracelsus: Life and Prophecies*, by Franz Hartmann, M.D., Steiner Books, Blauvelt, New York, 1973, p. 179.

[2] *The Hermetic and Alchemical Writings of Paracelsus*, edited by Arthur Edward Waite, Shambhala, Berkeley, Ca., 1976, vol. II, p. 286.

[3] Hartmann, *op. cit.*, p. 156.

[4] *The Secret of the Golden Flower*, Richard Wilhelm & C. G. Jung, Wehman Bros., New York, 1955, p. 112.

[5] *Collected Works*, C. G. Jung, Princeton University Press, Princeton, New Jersey, Vol. 10, para. 355.

[6] Waite, *op. cit.*, p. 272.

SATURN AND THE ART OF SEEING

The concept of alchemical lead as the stuff that was worked upon in an attempt to create gold is an idea familiar even to the most disinterested. It is in fact often enough used to define the primary concerns of alchemy by those who view this art as having been nothing more than an aberration of early chemistry. A cursory examination of alchemical literature reveals many intelligent and sincere alchemists — the greater majority of whom were physicians — expressing this belief in ways presently obscure to us. The lead they wrote of was not the common lead, no more than was the gold they repeatedly praised.

Their continued reference to Saturn as a synonym for this substance alerts us to the fact that what they spoke of was a particular type of experience rather than a specific substance, and that the lineaments of this experience can be found in the myths of Saturn. This paper will therefore concern itself with the mythological figure of Saturn in the belief that the image of this God at the very least expresses modalities of soul experience common to all of us.

In much the same way that the term "spiritual" limits our appreciation of processes common to our everyday experience, so too does the term "psychological" limit our appreciation of the processes whose mysteries have been reduced to the commonplace. The two terms stand at opposite poles and have come to symbolize viewpoints antagonistic to one another. I therefore prefer to employ the term "archetypal" in the firm belief that it not only defines the activities and conditions referred to by the terms psychological and spiritual, but that it also defines an experience in which the meanings of the two terms can be thought of as indistinguishable from one another. In former ages, a preliminary introduction to a discussion of a God would not have been necessary; nor would the defining of terms have been a prerequisite to such discussions. But we exist at a moment in history where certain phenomena can just as easily be described from a psychological point of view as from a spiritual or religious one. This convergence does not imply, as is more often than not taken to be the case, that one explanation nullifies the other. In fact it points us to the level at which the two perspectives are complementary. If these disciplines simply describe two sides of the same coin, then the coin itself defines a distinct reality in which spiritual and psychological facts simultaneously occur.

Furthermore, whereas psychological and spiritual activities are always described as taking place *in* a clearly defined space—the human mind on the one hand, heaven or the suprapersonal on the other—the archetypes, as Jung has pointed out, "are not found exclusively in the psychic sphere,"[1] but manifest themselves throughout the world. To follow Henry Corbin's lead, the archetype (and the archetypal world) "rather than being situated . . . situates, . . . is situating."[2] To be situated by Saturn, therefore, is to be contained in and working through certain Saturnian modes of being. But we no longer speak in a mythological tongue of experience, and while it is true that "mythology is a psychology of antiquity . . . psychology . . . a mythology of modernity,"[3] we are for the time being stuck with psychological language when describing archetypal experiences. As Jung put it, "Only an unparalleled impoverishment of symbolism could enable us to rediscover the gods as psychic factors, that is, as archetypes of the unconscious."[4] We might append to this that only an impoverishment of imaginal language as well could have caused the creation of psychological language.

Having made these statements about psychological language and implied that spiritual or mystical language no longer carries the weight necessary to engage the sceptic empiricist, I am left with the problem of finding a medium within which I can discuss Saturn. This medium would have to be one in which the impact of the archetype on life could be validated if not immediately experienced and seen. Because archetypes affect both the psychological and spiritual areas of life, and because both of these areas have given birth to the art of counselling in one form or another, I believe it would be best to speak of Saturn from the viewpoint of the counselor. But this type of counselor would have to be a peculiar blend of empiricist and metaphysician, having at his or her disposal a system whose very structure is archetypally given. In addition, the system would have to have as its structural base a clearcut connection to archetypal images, if not myths themselves, and it would have to derive its information solely from those images or symbols. Furthermore, it could not be recent, with origins far removed from the created ideographic realm of modern persons. In short, its authority would have to be a given, derived in much the manner that an archetype expresses itself. Admittedly, these qualifications could in part answer certain schools of psychological thought, and almost all religious counselling. But neither one of these forms of counselling rely solely on the archetypes for seeing. Both demand that a human story be told, each then seeking to fit that story within the mold of the image they believe the story fits. And, furthermore, neither one of them can claim to see an entire life as an archetypal structure which from moment to moment is effected by archetypes that can be specifically named. Finally, neither one can claim a long and intimate connection with the art by which imagined realities could be revealed and worked upon: the art of alchemy.

The form of counselling that appears to fit all of the above requirements is astrology. I cannot here argue the reasons why astrology does indeed work,[5] but must ask my reader at least to allow that as a counselling tool it can be as effective as any other. I will therefore speak of it as an art that still affords us the greatest possibility for speaking an archetypal language that includes both psychological and spiritual perspectives.

*   *   *

The most familiar description of Kronus is given us in Hesiod's creation myth, the *Theogony*. The tale informs us that the Great Mother, Gaia, came into being first and created the limits of the known world, along with the Titans, Cyclopes, and her own brother-husband, Uranos. Uranos came to her daily for sexual union, refusing to allow the children born of these unions to issue from her body. She in time grew weary of his sexual demands along with the burden of her imprisoned children. Petitioning her children to aid her in her plight, Kronos came forth armed with a sickle given him by his mother and emasculated his father, tossing the severed genitals into the ocean. Kronos then took over rulership and fathered the pantheon that would in time rule the world: Zeus, Hera, Poseidon, Demeter, Hestia, and Hades. Warned that one of his children would supplant him, he took to swallowing them as soon as they were born. His wife, Rhea, tiring of her husband's demands, hid the infant Zeus from his father. Once grown, Zeus battled with Kronos for the throne and after successfully defeating him banished the old ruler to Tartaros, a dark region believed to be beneath Hades itself, so distant that an anvil dropped from the surface of the earth would fall for nine days before reaching his father's final prison.

The manner by which Kronos was defeated is worth considering. Zeus asked the Titaness, Metis (Wise Council or Insight), to aid him in the administration of an emetic to his father. After swallowing, Kronos vomited up Zeus' brothers and sisters — the Olympians who from that time forward would reign from above, if not from the sky itself.

What we are more than likely witness to in this particular tale is the personification of the type of shift in consciousness that occurs anytime a culture moves from a meteorologically-based calendar to one purely astronomical. One could here phantasize that the seasonal calendar, in that it grew out of simple observations of the immediately felt cycles of change occurring in Nature, gave rise to the myths of the Great Mother and her dying and resurrecting consorts. More than likely the initial calendric myths would have arisen from the simple movements of the Sun and Moon. With more detailed observation of these two bodies the shift from a seasonal to an astronomical calendar began to occur. A meteorological calendar demands nothing more than simple observation. The cycle of the seasons signifies when to plant, when to harvest, when to store up provisions. That is, consciousness need little exert itself; need do nothing more than attend to what is happening before one's eyes and upon the land. The shift towards a calendar founded upon astronomical events would have demanded not only a focusing of attention on phenomena removed from one's immediate perception, but the creation of a notational system as complex as the movements it recorded. The sudden emergence of sky gods where once earth goddesses reigned probably mirrors such an event. This new type of attention, this honing of a consciousness that once attended only to the immediacy of phenomena, was the seed of abstract and philosophical thought.

Furthermore, the tendency of the deep psyche to personify phenomena, that same tendency which originally allowed the earth to be seen and experienced as female, as Great Mother, continued in its propensity, now identifying the sky with the Great Father and the male. Thus, this shift into a new modality of consciousness at first not only became identified with the masculine but would in time become a synonym for consciousness. Such personifications still exist and are the very stuff of those psychological theories that personify the realms now called consciousness and the unconscious. We therefore find Freud writing that the "motive force of repression in each individual is a struggle between the two sexual characters. The dominant sex of the person, that which is the more strongly developed, has repressed the mental representation of the subordinated sex into the unconscious. Therefore the nucleus of the unconscious (that is to say, the repressed) is in each human being that side of him which belongs to the opposite sex. . . . To put the theory briefly: with men, what is unconscious and repressed can be reduced to feminine instinctual impulses; and conversely with women."[6]

One is forced to ask what exactly is a feminine instinctual impulse, and what a masculine? Is Freud saying that what is repressed in a male, what the ego cannot bear, *becomes* identified as feminine, in a woman masculine? That is, does the very existence of the thing called feminine or masculine depend upon experiences or material that consciousness has denied, has repressed? Is the term "feminine" assigned by a male to a thing he cannot allow of himself, "masculine" that which a woman cannot — and is what each cannot allow solely dictated by social convention, or is it a deep innate propensity to project onto a distinctly other being what is negatively experienced in them? Do our concepts of the masculine and the feminine come into existence through repression first, and then by projection?

Let me come at it from another direction: *whatever* an individual finds intolerable to their psychic stability, is that the stuff that they then project onto the opposite sex? Is the concept of the masculine and the feminine a myth, a projection, nothing more than the display of the deep psyche's tendency to personify? And does such personification demand images of extreme difference, creating self by hostility to an imagined other? Listen to the psychological imaginings of the Jungian Erich Neumann:

> Consciousness . . . is masculine even in women, just as the unconscious is feminine in men . . . it is consistent with the conscious-unconscious structure of the opposites that the unconscious should be regarded as predominantly feminine, and consciousness as predominantly masculine. This correlation is self-evident, because the unconscious, alike in its capacity to bring to birth and to destroy through absorption, has feminine affinities. The feminine is conceived mythologically under the aspect of this archetype; uroboros and Great Mother are both feminine dominants, and all the psychic constellations over which they rule are under the dominance of the unconscious. Conversely, its opposite, the system of ego consciousness, is masculine. With it are associated the qualities of volition, decision, and activity as contrasted with the determinism and blind 'drives' of the preconscious, egoless state."[7]

Here we are told that the feminine is that which creates and destroys, blind, without ego, and compelled; masculine, that which is decisive, volatile, active and in control. Whereas in Freud the qualities of the feminine and the masculine are determined by their repression, here in Neumann's mythology neither male nor female would want anything to do with the feminine. Is this not the stuff of Hesiodic, Kronian mythology? What is "self-evident" to Neumann is that the unconscious is blind and that the thing called ego is no different from its forerunner in our myth of Kronos.

Both Freud and Neumann reveal personifications of the first

order. Jung, in attempting to clarify the matter towards the end of his life, corrects his original position, the one from which Neumann took his lead, by stating that by identifying "Sol with consciousness and Luna with the unconscious, we would now be driven to the conclusion that a woman cannot possess a consciousness."[8] He goes on to say, "The error in our formulation lies in the fact, firstly, that we equated the moon with the unconscious as such, whereas the equation is true chiefly of the unconscious in man; and secondly, that we overlooked the fact that the moon is not only dark but is also a giver of light and can therefore represent consciousness. This is indeed so in the case of woman: her consciousness has a lunar rather than a solar character."[9]

Here too, while nonetheless carried by a more democratic phantasy, the personifying character of the psyche is present, for we are at the same time informed that this lunar character "does not show up objects in all their pitiless discreteness and separateness, like the harsh, glaring light of day, but blends in a deceptive shimmer the near and the far, magically transforming little things into big things, high into low, softening all colour into a bluish haze, and blending the nocturnal landscape into an unsuspected unity."[10]

So, here we are told that the feminine, or at least the consciousness of women, is a dim light that *deceptively* merges the differences of opposites into a unity, somehow temporarily relieving us of the real essence of objects. As in the myth of Ge and Uranus, Rhea and Kronos, the feminine is deceptive, a betrayer. And the masculine? An over-bearing nit-picker. Psychology is as subject to these personifying qualities of deep psyche as the old mythology. No matter how far along this road of consciousness we may continually pride ourselves in having advanced, we are left with the bothersome possibility that every perception, every insight, will in time (as history has shown) be discovered to have to some degree been riveted with projections. This is what Jung meant when he said that the unconscious is inexhaustible: the base of the human soul, for want of another phrase, is *potentia*—a tree of eternal life comprised of our continued need to know, to understand, to be certain. And here we see why a symbol contains all the information needed for its decipherment, why nothing need be added to the image, for the image, whether it be presented by a mythographer from the fifth century B.C. or the twentieth century

A.D., carries with it every imaginable hook needed for any human projection. It is by such hooks, through such engagements, that we strive to free ourselves from the personifying tendencies of the soul — tendencies that ultimately give shape to a thing we call the unconscious.

To return to our opening description of the theogonic myth, we have in the figure of Kronos the cast of liberator first, devourer second, and vanquished third. We also have in the name Kronos the idea that the God creates time divisions — he delineates beginning, middle and end. Thus, every Kronos time has these three qualities. Whereas Uranos knew no limit but continually set about the business of creation without end, Kronos brings a close to eternal creation. In short, he constitutes the first phenomenon peculiar to being in this world. He is the father of our experience *in* being. When I am pressed for time, fear its loss, suffer its interminable passage, wonder where it went, then I know the full meaning of Kronos as an oppressive power. Kronos limits and therefore defines the experience of life, thus he becomes the archetype of history. Kronos destroys the creative principle of the father in order to liberate. We might psychologize this and say that my cutting free of the constraining influence of father at the parental and societal level allows those qualities that I was born with to come into the light of day, into consciousness.

Murray Stein has pointed out that this Creation tale corrects the Freudian supposition that the male child fears castration by the father.[11] Here, it is quite simply indicated that it is the father who fears castration by the son. Castration is de-meaning, a depowering that leads to the father's fall. This re-sighting of the Freudian myth of Oedipus leads to some startling implications.

Freud informs us that it is the young male's fear of castration that leads to an initial experience of guilt, which in turn gives rise to the establishment of the super-ego — a structure created by the internalization of the father principle contained in both the real father and society. With the image of the castrating son instead of the Freudian castrating father, castration becomes a vehicle for the establishment of the young Heroic ego. Here, Saturn becomes a creator or liberator of a new form of consciousness, a consciousness that sets a limit upon the fecundity of the primal psyche we carry within. It stops the psyche's original desire, easily witnessed in young children, to act on impulse, even compulsively. Kronos/

Saturn is the element that halts play, teaching the child that there must be a limit to the desire to fulfill its pleasures in every given moment. Thus, Kronos symbolizes the quality in consciousness that is capable of interrupting, suppressing, repressing, and redirecting the spontaneous and instinctual. And it does this for the purpose of meeting and maintaining the demand for order that is peculiar to the human experience. I refer to this as Spiritualization, defining the process as the limiting effect of ego on that which is without ego or non-ego.

The next image that the tale of Kronos presents is the son becoming the father: no sooner am I freed of that which parents and constrains me than I become parent and constrainer. I then devour my own children, my own creativity and potential, and even my own future. Kronos is one who would turn every experience into a father-experience, allowing no change of rules, always telling us that the right way to go about things has been left us by the past. Kronos is against materia, against body, against nature. He is the defining spirit of an age, of the time, of the moment.

Psychologically, the entire myth reads as follows: Uranos, the sky, would keep or locate all creative potentials in matter, the stuff of the world. It would seek to materialize and concretize every new idea. It would take every spontaneous creative thought and make it practical and earthbound. It would accomplish this through perpetual penetration of earthly matters and concerns, refusing to let go of its mater/matter. Kronos frees such potential by castration. So is the psyche ensnared in the tendency to materialize or literalize, freed up and allowed to come into the light of day. But now this creative energy, having seen the light of consciousness, becomes ensnared in Kronos—by the limits of spiritualization. Its function now is to nourish spirit, the paternal, dogma, institutions, and ego. What eventually releases the constraining power of this Saturnian energy is insight, the application of Metis. That is, by in-sighting, by penetrating to the belly of the archetype, we liberate the powers it imprisons.

Everything that I have presented up to this point concerning Kronos fits within parameters of both psychology and astrology. It is at just this point where one is tempted to make of the two arts one, to in fact relate the Kronos figure of mythology to the psychology of C.G. Jung, in particular to the structure and dynamics of the human psyche. However, to do so would be to ignore the fact that Jung himself stated that the archetypes transcend the human psyche, an idea more in accord with the ancient theories of astrology than the modern attempt to legitimize astrology by turning it into a psychology, a *science* of soul rather than an *art*. This drive towards "scientific" respectability on the part of astrology — a drive that psychology itself became victim to not too long ago — serves to do nothing more than deprecate valuable ideas that astrology originally held. What we fail to see in such an effort is that if in making a thing respectable we must divorce ourselves from the past then we become the castrating Kronos ourselves on the one hand, and the devourer of all that is potential in soul on the other. And here I specifically refer to the fact that the planets of astrology were once understood as Gods — not psychological co-ordinates. Our present inability to accept such an idea grows out of our failure to experience myth.

Simply put, myth refers us to a dimension residing beside and beyond the lineaments of what we usually identify as reality. It was once the tale of the Gods, of powers whose phantastic and improbable natures when viewed through the rationalism of the twentieth century, could only exist, if they exist at all, in imagination. We think of myth as something antiquity has left us, of something once believed in but no longer tenable. Myth more often than not is deemed little more than the fancy shadow of what was once considered a reality. We today in the West pride ourselves in knowing that it is certain atmospheric conditions that give cause to thunder and lightning, not the great God Zeus; that what causes panic or hysteria is a psychological difficulty and not the God Pan; that love simply comes about because of a series of mutual attractions and compatibilities, and not the God Eros. When we look at myth we see it as nothing more than a system of metaphors pacifying the scientific ignorance of our ancestors.

What we fail to appreciate concerning these ancestors and their myths is the immediacy of the phenomena portrayed. The image of Zeus was not created in an attempt to explain thunder and lightning, but rather was the spontaneous representation of an emotional response to thunder and lightning. To see myth as nothing more than a series of metaphors is to assume that myth is a logical construct, a product of pure intellect. Myth alludes to the affect accompanying a specific reality which in the final analysis is undecipherable except in terms of the image. Myth, if nothing else, is the record of an unreferable experience.

The experiences that gave birth to these mythic images still occur, but today we have a different set of terms to define them — transpersonal or transcendent, altered states of consciousness, hypnogogic, or hallucinatory. What is of interest in all of these is that they distance us from such experiences by locating them in a realm outside or above so-called normal consciousness. But what we today call "normal consciousness" is actually a quality of perception defined by the influence of logical positivism or empiricism. We forget that we are not born empiricists but trained to perceive and experience reality from such a vantage point. While an empirical approach to the phenomenal world is critical for the differentiation and classification of phenomena, when it is used to define our immediate and felt experience the danger of splitting ourselves off from the other dynamic factors of the soul becomes very real. This type of thinking leads to the creation of ego-psychologies that seek to standardize human experience.

But if we remind ourselves of what Jung said concerning the archetypes — that they pass through, include and affect soul, but are not its property — then we are left with the fact that the archetypes not only work on something else, but also perform this work *somewhere else*. The first and most apparent place is in nature itself. The other place we shall speak of shortly. What all of this implies is that the person is not the center of the cosmos: that the person is, in fact, something that must be connected to the cosmos. What psychology presently attempts to do, and I suspect much of astrological counseling, is to separate the person from the cosmos by insisting that consciousness is the significator of an ultimate reality.

This humanizing of the archetypes in both psychology and astrology becomes blatantly apparent when we turn to the concept of soul. Invariably, we speak of "my soul," ignoring the fact that early philosophy spoke of "the soul," or the *anima mundi* or world soul. It was believed that the entire universe was contained in such a soul, and that we were each allotted a small portion of that larger soul to work upon in our lives. But where in either psychology or astrology is there work done on the world soul? Nowhere that I can see. And where in either psychology or astrology do we not relate soul to life, earthly life, my life, the life of the individual and of persons? In short, what has happened to *this* archetype? Obviously, in attending to the problem of making lives astrological and psychological, we have cut ourselves off from what is fully archetypal.

We might arrive at a clearer picture of this original soul principle if we turn to the zodiacal figure of astrology — that figure which portrays the ideal relationship of the elements, signs, houses and planets to each other. This zodiacal figure is what was once referred to as the world soul, or the grand person. What is curious about this figure is that no human being alive in either past, present or future could ever have a horoscope like it. That is, my horoscope fails to hit the mark of archetypal wholeness, revealing where I have fallen short of this wholeness. Because this zodiacal figure, or archetype of wholeness, always lurks behind every horoscope, astrological counseling becomes an attempt to perform the impossible: to lead the person in the direction of this wholeness. Psychology does much the same with its concept of "normalcy" or wholeness.

In astrology, the natal chart (in psychology the circumstances of life) becomes the focus of attention. Both types of data are employed in an attempt to regulate or normalize the individual. In each instance the attempt is to see what the problem in an individual life is, and how it can either be corrected or compensated. In astrology, therefore, we find ourselves dealing with two dimensions. The first is that depicted in the natal chart: the given of a life, that is to say, the particulars of my history. The second is the psychological: to what degree the physical realities have impaired or enhanced my psychology. Where is the blockage and where is the flow? The theory of the archetypes can be very helpful here, for we often point to exactly how and when I have been affected by an archetype — but it is limited, for it leaves out a third dimension of the person.

This dimension appears to have been forgotten by both astrology on the whole, and psychology in part, and is what the alchemist Paracelsus referred to when he wrote that there is a double system of stars. There are the stars without and the stars within. In order for the outward Saturn to have any effect on me, it must work through the inner Saturn.[12] Paracelsus adds that between the two star systems there exists a medium star zone — thus his famous dictum that "Imagination is the star in man." It is through the medium of imagination that we are capable of bringing forth a new heaven.[13] In another work he informs us that "he which would perfect this art [alchemy] must, as it were, build a new world."[14] In other words, in order to create the Philosopher's Stone, one first must create a new world through the use of imagination.

If we read the alchemists carefully, especially the papers collected by Elias Ashmole in his *Theatrum Chemicum Britannicum*, it becomes clear that this Philosopher's Stone comes into being by following an astrological schedule and that the Stone answers the description of the zodiacal archetype, the *anima mundi*, or perfect person. Thus, the astrological wholeness imaged by the zodiacal archetype can be created by an individual: it is apparent what is being alluded to here is the subtle body. It is just here that things start to become difficult for us in the modern world, for what is being suggested is that we can create an ephemeral body, a personality capable of existing after the body's death. In addition, this body is created out of no-thing, out of air to all appearances, and it has an independent life of its own both in and out of human existence. Before we scoff at this idea, it would do us well to consider some modern theories of psychology.

A case in point is the theory of the ego. Psychology in general agrees that the ego is not a given — it is not fully present in the infant — but a thing created over the course of the years. In time it becomes the center of consciousness, even identified with consciousness. There is no denying that a psychic substance has been made, created, out of no-thing. This ephemeral body is the child of all western psychologies.

Jung, the creator of the psychological term "complex," has pointed out that the ego is a complex, a complex being defined as a grouping of psychic elements about emotionally toned-contents, a nuclear psychic element around which associations cluster. The term is most familiar to us in such phrases as "mother-complex" or "father-complex," referring us to psychological states in which an individual is engaged or identified with the parent in question to the point where it is detrimental to his or her autonomy as an individual. The ego, being but one of many complexes, may also offer such dangers as can be seen in individuals one would label as being "egotistical." The peculiar feature of complexes that are unconscious, beyond the immediate and willed reach of consciousness, is that they may each form a personality of their own. A complex,

Jung tells us, is a sort of body that can upset the stomach, breathing, and the heart. He likens a complex to a partial personality, pointing out that it is the source of those personalities that appear in schizophrenia.[15]

The picture that we have to this point is of a field of consciousness containing at an idealized center a created psychic body or complex, called the ego. This picture on the other hand tells us that in the unconscious there are any number of other complexes possible—each having an independent life of its own. The ego and these other complexes appear to be spontaneous phenomena. They *happen to us*. Psychology has shown that we can work on these complexes, especially the ego—that a certain amount of willing and attention can alter their basic natures.

Now let me propose this: if it is possible for us to create greater and more substantial properties of this ephemeral thing called the ego, is there not the possibility that we can also create yet another psychic body? And may not this psychic body or complex be the very thing that the ancients and the alchemists referred to as the subtle body of the Stone? If we can create another psychic body, similar in substance and composition to the ego, where then would it reside? One is tempted to equate the place where such a subtle body might take shape as the unconscious itself. But it must be noted that the heaven Paracelsus speaks of is created by imagination: that is, it is something created by the person. The unconscious exists, *it is*, there is no need for us to create it. This other dimension or level or place is composed of imagination and imaginal substances. It is *the* imaginal. This is the dimension of the horoscope, I propose, that has been forgotten: this is the place where the world soul exists, the place where I can become re-connected with the cosmos. Whereas our psychologies tell us we must work on consciousness, ego, and the unconscious, this place need not be worked on. It need only be attended to, allowed admittance into our lives. What happens at this third dimension of the horoscope happens outside of the space/time continuum. It is an archetypal dimension, a place of powers existing beyond the human. The home of the Gods, if you will.

What I am suggesting here is that we are affected by a dimension that has nothing to do with personality development, ego growth, or the expansion of consciousness. What it has to do with is connections, archetypal connections. In both astrology and psychology there is an attitude that one must be strengthened, made better, developed. So we take what we are and we attempt to transform ourselves, become better, whole, palpable. But, I ask you, is there the possibility that what has been given *is* something of value in its own right. And is there the possibility that my experience of archetypal or astrological wholeness might be possible at this imaginal level? We are continually attempting to fit the zodiacal archetype at the personal level—something that is an impossibility—but might not this other dimension of psyche be the very place where it is achieved?

Let me define these three dimensions before moving on: the first would be the place where physical adjustments are made to what has been given; the second would refer us to the psychological work and adjustment that must be made to what is given; and the third would be working on what I am as *given*, without any attempt to alter or modify. The work of this last dimension is an imaginal work. The involvement with what has been given is the stuff of souls. I change nothing, attempt to make nothing better, but perceive "it" as it is in the hope of discerning in it an archetypal meaning that will deepen my perception of life. This would imply that one of the functions of astrology (as well as of psychology) would be involved not with the art of counseling but with the art of seeing, or with the art of revealing—for no other purpose than to see myself clearly as I am. The objective would be not to correct, but literally to objectify; not to expand but to deepen. What is now counseling would become witnessing. The astrologer and the psychologist would aid me in the problem of discovering what I am. Transformation would be discussed not in terms of making something better out of what one has, but in being what one is.

In his book *Re-Visioning Psychology*, James Hillman has defined soul as "a perspective rather than a substance, a viewpoint toward things rather than a thing itself. This perspective is reflective, it mediates events and makes differences between ourselves and everything that happens. Between us and the events, between the doer and the deed, there is a reflective moment—and the soul-making means differentiating this middle ground."[16] The middle ground Hillman refers us to is the medium of imagination that for Paracelsus exists between the stars above and the stars within. It is by differentiating this middle ground, this imaginal dimension, that one connects oneself with nature and the cosmos. Our next question is, how is this to be done? What is the method of soul-making, or reconnecting?

Jung re-discovered one way we might become again engaged, actively, with the archetypal realm. He called this active imagination; it is a short-cut to the unconscious, which entails "the releasing of unconscious processes and letting them come into the conscious mind in the form of fantasies . . ." not "giving priority to understanding" them.[17] Libido, or psychic energy, can only be consciously apprehended and joined to consciousness through the image.[18] The objective of this technique was the bringing over of so-called inferior functions into consciousness for the purpose of transforming them, thus enhancing consciousness. In yet another paper he informs us that psychic processes might be thought of as a scale along which consciousness slides.[19] He likens one end of the scale to the pure instinctual impulse, the other to the image of that impulse or the archetype. To come into contact with the image or archetype, rather than to fall into the compulsive area of the instinct, one need only perform active imagination. In other words, the image is father of the action. Hillman writes that "any transformation of the images affects the patterns of behavior."[20]

The purpose behind the method of active imagination, originally, was that of creating a greater field of consciousness, or bringing things over from the archetypal realm into consciousness. But there is a new suggestion in Jungian psychology that states we must go beyond active imagination into archetypal imagination. The thesis behind this is that active imagination—a process that demands the person performing the imagination include themselves in the images produced, guiding and entering them as they develop—limits the experience of the archetypal or imaginal. What we get ultimately is the story of the imaginer himself. The focus of archetypal imagination would be nothing less than a rooting in that which is beyond psyche, that which the ancients referred to as heaven.[21]

Jung wrote that active imagination in time produces a third thing, "a living birth that leads to a new level of being, a new situation."[22] This is the new world or body that the ancients and the alchemists told us we are capable of forming. By creating this new thing, we truly participate in the work of nature, we somehow affect nature and transform it, making of it not an evolutionary phenomenon, but a revolutionary happening.

I have led you down this road in an attempt to shed light on my statement that the purpose of engaging with the imaginal realm, the archetypal reality, is to become active participants in the transformation of nature. Not *our* natures, but nature itself. This is the real meaning of transformation—it is not person-centered, it is archetypally centered and it is a way in which we may all contribute to the ever-unfolding work of Genesis. The materials of the ancient art of astrology constitute a method by which this may be achieved. In addition to the counselling that the horoscope appears to engender, there is this third work that every astrologer should concern himself with: working with the *image* of the horoscope itself.

My horoscope shows me exactly where and how the imaginal has become enmeshed with me, where the gods have taken on new characteristics, new problems. My horoscope is the continuation of written myth, it is the tale not only of myself, but of the Gods in their evolution in imaginal time and space, their individuation.

The horoscope might therefore be thought of as an active imagination performed by the Gods, or the planets, or whatever you wish to call these powers that shape us. The new function of the astrologer would be to engage me at this archetypal level by having me perform an archetypal imagination on my horoscope. This would entail not an hour of understanding or interpretation, but an hour of story-telling. The astrologer would tell me the story of the particular God-planets, and then point out exactly where my horoscope coincides with the original tale. Then we, the two of us, would engage in a conversation outlining the development of the myths as revealed by the differences in my horoscope. The horoscope would become not just a tool through which I understand myself, but a method by which I can see myself as a part of a larger whole. Instead of a broadening and enlargement of consciousness, this would be a deepening and engagement with soul.

The corpus of texts known as the *Hermetica* has the following:

> Leap clear of all that is corporeal, and make yourself grow to a like expanse with that greatness which is beyond all measure: rise above all time, and become eternal: then you will apprehend God. Think that for you too nothing is impossible: deem that you too are immortal, and that you are able to grasp all things in your thought . . . find you a home in the haunts of every living

creature: make yourself higher than all heights, and lower than all depths: bring together in yourself all opposites of quality, heat and cold, dryness and fluidity; think that you are everywhere at once, grasp in your thought all this at once, all times and places, all substances and qualities and magnitudes together: then you can apprehend God."[23]

This clearly refers us to the art of archetypal imagination. The horoscope of the individual is the rocket that allows the person access to this other dimension of experience. The images contained therein are not just psychological qualities, but the Gods themselves as they exist at the periphery of the human world. The horoscope is a field of imagination and reflection not only through which we see ourselves, but by which we see *through* ourselves to the archetypal ground that has created this dance we call life.

Now I must turn you to the next question. What is it that caused us to lose sight of this level of astrological work? Why have we failed to see that the horoscope is not only a way into ourselves, but a way out of ourselves as well, into the greater drama we all carry about or are carried about in? The answer, to my way of thinking, is the God Saturn.

Consider this: the restraining and repressing of the children by Uranos might be likened to the early stages of primacy when the elements that will in time compose the ego are refused light of day. Assuredly, these are primitive aspects of ego—the monsters of childhood imagination. Saturn at first releases these elements from the belly of the unconscious, only in time to devour the newer and controlling aspects of ego in the form of his children. Everything in consciousness now becomes spiritualized and controlled. If these elements are to have any expression at all, it must be through the father, through paternal law. The new heaven, Olympus, can come into being only through the release of these children who will in time rule the world. I suggest here that the new heaven, the Olympus, is the imaginal heaven of Paracelsus, the reflective ground of soul that Hillman refers us to, and the deeper level of the horoscope. The only thing that will allow us to create this heaven in both astrology and psychology is the application of an elixir by in-sight. In short, the only way we can release ourselves from Saturn's tendency to spiritualize and intellectualize the cosmos and the imaginal is by in-sighting, or seeing into the imaginal through the mirror of the horoscope.

If there is any one idea I am trying to put forward, it is that we must resuscitate a forgotten function of astrology that allows the reunion of the person with the imaginal, the creation of a subtle body, and the continuance of Genesis. All of this may be accomplished by the re-instatement of a way of seeing with the eyes of the soul.

We must delve deeper into the tale of Kronos, filling out the little details. To begin with, the Uranian difficulty is one that directs all energy into creating stuff from mater — from materia — and filling matter up. Uranian consciousness is a *participation mystique* with the world and with matter. It is a limited consciousness in that it sees nothing but what lies in front of it. The next stage in the development of consciousness is marshalled in by Kronos. He liberates through curtailment of the instinctual and the impulsive.

Kronos then imposes limitations upon his own children by swallowing them. That is, he does not let them remain in matter. He allows the creative issue of his seed into the light of day for a moment before incorporating them in his own body. Instead of a consciousness that works through the body of materia/mother, a making of the world, we now have a consciousness that spiritualizes or intellectualizes the world as well as the instincts or impulses. If energy is to express itself, it must do so in a controlled manner. Kronos is a consciousness that has no contact with either the unconscious or the instinctual. Every impulse, and therefore every creative upsurge, becomes swallowed up.

At first, the containment of all these children appears to be nothing more than a legitimate limitation of things. We today tend to admire the Kronos figure operating in this manner. We say limitation is a necessary quality of life, a function of a good ego. To become whole is to become aware consciously of one's limitations. It is just here where astrological and psychological counselling can itself become Saturnian: by turning all patterns of behavior that do not fit the archetypal model of wholeness into vehicles of transformation; in whatever is difficult or unsavory, we must somehow find something good, and in order to create the good we must obviously have some kind of model of the good. This is the process of spiritualization that Kronos/Saturn adores.

We have already noted Jung's perception that whereas modern persons do not have direct communication with the Gods, the Gods now manifest themselves to us through our illnesses — be such illness physical or psychological.[24] He writes elsewhere that whenever he was confronted with a crisis or major difficulty in life, he invariably found God behind it all. Therefore, to cure ourselves of our illness or our difficulties, to make of the dark stuff of life good stuff and healthiness, is also to rid ourselves of the God in the darkness. To take the difficult image of Kronos/Saturn and manage to find in his demands goodness and reasonableness, is to never know Saturn *as he is*. What we end up knowing is his effect, his mercurial, tricksterish process of spiritualization. This is how Saturn limits us: by not allowing us to experience him as he is. There is a darkness to this god, and he cannot be experienced without it.

The function of Kronos/Saturn is to instruct us in the nature of limitation, depression, and the dryness of a wisdom that seeks to make all things equal. Dryness is the nature of ego, but Heraclitus tells us that, "It is delight, or rather death, to souls to become wet . . ."[25] and that "to souls, it is death to become water: to water it is death to become earth, from earth comes water, and from water, soul."[26] The dry wisdom of the wise old man Saturn is soul become spirit. As Heraclitus points out, it is death to water (soul) to become earth, to become the psychological matter of consciousness and the ego. But life is earth become water, for from water comes soul.

This is a loaded statement when we compare it to the castration in our tale. Uranos, the one totally and purely involved in mater/matter, has his genitals thrown into the ocean by his son Kronos. Hesiod informs us that the castrated member floats upon the ocean for a long time, foam gathering about it, bearing inside it the immortal being who shall soon be spawned—Aphrodite, goddess of love, the "foam born." So it begins: the compulsive sexual engagement of Uranos with his wife Gaia, when prevented—when cut off —leads to the birth of love. Note that it is not sexuality and love that are equated here. What is implied is that behind every compulsive act, there is a seed of love that can emerge if one can cut oneself off from impulsivity.

What is it that accomplishes the end of compulsion? It is this: the limitation of Kronos, the demand that we do not concretize and make physical certain deep inner promptings. What is born of water and defunct genitals is the first image of soul. The message is: the way to soul comes only after putting an end to the concretizing of instinct and the casting of all our energy "out there" into the world. But Kronos does not see or know of this, for Hesiod tells us that he threw his father's genitals behind him, over his shoulder. In short, he failed to see the value concealed in both instinct and compulsion. This is the stuff that Kronos limits by keeping his children away from the feminine, in his own body.

Therefore, the counsellor working with the image of Kronos is faced with two dangers. The first is in not fully appreciating that the limiting effect of Kronos on compulsions and instincts is only good in and for itself if one looks behind the God. The second danger is in failing to see that this statement refers to the physical level alone. In the imaginal realm, at the deepest level of soul, we must experience Kronian blindness if we are to experience love. It is only because Kronos does not see what is contained in the genitals of his father that Aphrodite is born. If he had seen it, he more than likely would have spiritualized the event, making of Aphrodite a Virgin Mary, which she is far from being.

Lucretius, in his work *On the Nature of Things*, informs us that Aphrodite is always accompanied by wild beasts in hot desire. She is the mistress of Ares (Mars in astrology), the God of war, the first being to be tried for murder. Thus, Aphrodite is joined with murderous passion. In that she is the mother of Phobos (fear) and Deimos (terror), it is also implied that every act of love is capable of producing these experiences. As for the god who is her legal husband, Hephaestus, he is a lame blacksmith whom the Gods found comical—his feet were turned backwards. All of which is to say that Aphrodite's divinity is compensated for by that which is *crippled*. In addition, she worried her husband with numerous affairs—another way of saying that in every loving there is the potential for deceit. This is no valentine-card goddess of love, but a deceptively pleasing-to-look-at power capable of reducing us to the level of fools. This fact is nicely depicted on a gem talisman from the Graeco-Roman period. The description of the talisman is contained in the following spell:

> Take a magnetic stone . . . design on it Aphrodite riding Psyche as on horseback, holding her with the left hand and doing up the locks of her hair. Below Aphrodite, and Psyche, Eros, standing upright on a globe: he holds a lighted torch with which he burns Psyche . . . on the other side of the stone, Eros and Psyche embracing.

On another gem, Syrian in origin, we find the same scene, the obverse side depicting the two lovers kissing above the inscription "Curable love-wound."[27]

The figure of Psyche, a mortal maiden who first appears in the tale of Amor and Psyche, refers us to what we now call the human psyche. On this talisman she is depicted under the dominion of Aphrodite, reduced to the state of an animal, a beast of the burden of Aphroditic love. In short, the soul is represented in the service of the instinctual and compulsive side of loving, for Aphrodite is the goddess who inspires love of her, not of another. The intensity of the service and submission is symbolized by the burning torch of Eros, which on the coin is placed directly beneath Psyche's genitals. In other words, the purely erotic and instinctual ground of being rides the soul, bareback, while gazing into a mirror. The psyche is here at the beck and call of Aphroditic love with every pull of the instinctual reins. One is inflamed by the burning torch of Eros, and driven by Aphroditic self-involvement.

I am indebted to Prof. Donald Sheehan for telling me that the tale of *Amor and Psyche* was the last to be created by the Classical world before its downfall. This to me implies that the final message of the Classical world had to do with the nature of the soul and the phenomenon of loving. In that the obverse side of the coin mentioned above shows Eros and Psyche in close embrace, with the motto, "Curable love-wound," it is implied that this compulsive quality of Aphrodite is a necessary road. And it is a road that we today in our psychologies and counselling tend to advise people against, for it smacks of pathology. Yet, the figure of Aphrodite, if taken as an archetypal reality, informs us that she is on the side of the nature of loving: the drive element of the divine beast.

It is unsightly, ungainly, perhaps even a little frightening to some of us—but who amongst us have not experienced if not in reality, at least in phantasy, this seemingly unconscious and uncivilized call to be ridden, driven, and burned by love? If Saturn in the tale had seen what was contained in the compulsion of his father, this experience would have been spiritualized to the point that it is today in the East. There we find the figures of the divine in ecstatic copulation, suggesting that what is sexual in us is divine. And so it is to a point. But this particular attribute of making divine what is mortal, devalues the mortal. What is mortal, basic, and perhaps bestial, comes to be unacceptable unless it can be uplifted by a God-concept. When we view the sexual figures of the Orient, we allow ourselves the aesthetic privilege of finding what is pornographic in the West to be divine in the East. This is Kronos spiritualizing again. The inability to accept what is basic and base in humanity leads to a false aesthetics. Thus, the reason we have such a thing as pornography in the West — the graphic description of what Aphrodite is capable of demanding of us — is because Kronos did not see what was hidden in his father's compulsion. And it is just as well, for the issue of pornography is that it shows us realities we would rather deny on the one hand, while also revealing the extent to which humanity is capable of going with itself.

Now we must ask ourselves what is the difference between the compulsion of Uranos and that which is born of his genitals. At first sight they are the same, but the initial compulsion is materialistic in that it involves itself only with self-gratification, penetration of the world for one's own ends. Nothing comes of this other than power over the world. The compulsion of Uranos leads to a love of the concrete, accumulation of wealth, a filling up with possessions. Aphrodite on the other hand, can lead us beyond ourselves, to the other, and through the other reduce us, teach us that we alone are not the power. Her message is that the power resides in and through us, sometimes attacking through our genitals — for Aphrodite in classical times was the Goddess, obviously, of the genitals. More important, whereas in the first instance we may be reduced to her pack animal, if we are capable of enduring the trials that she imposes on the soul, we eventually gain union with Eros — with the loving void of compulsion. Kronos would keep us from that if he could. There are obviously instances when an individual in his or her chart displays a Kronian limitation in a variety of life situations. What then? Should one try to help them get past, around, or through the difficulty? Should one say, this is good for obviously you needed to be limited in this part of your life? Or should one instead say, go with the limitation to its fullest? Don't fight against it. It is what you are: see where *what you are* takes you.

I would choose the latter course, for to struggle against what you are is never to know fully what or who you are. The limitation of Kronos is a dark difficulty not to be got rid of by finding in it the gift of consciousness and courage, but rather by trusting that in your particular prison you will find what in you is separate and particular, what in you is individual and defining, what in you is explicitly yours, not to be shared with any other. To turn the darkness of Kronos into a "good" thing is to never experience the full nature of an archetype that suggests the dark night of the soul is the beginning of wholeness at the imaginal level. It is for this reason that Meister Eckhart wrote of Saturn as the dark purger who "in the heaven of the soul . . . becomes of angelic purity, bringing as reward the vision of God,"[28] and an alchemist wrote that "as lead burns up and resolves all the imperfections of the metals . . . so likewise tribulations in this life cleanse us from the many blemishes which we have incurred: wherefore St. Ambrose called it the key of heaven."[29]

But what of the loss of the Kronian rule in the tale of Hesiod? How does this come about and what is its meaning? As we mentioned earlier, Zeus caused Metis (insight) to administer an emetic to the God. Again, we find a water creature in a crucial role: Metis was the daughter of Oceanus — and obviously an aspect of soul according to the definition of Heraclitus. Zeus was later to swallow Metis, and thus for all eternity be capable of thinking and speaking with insight and wise counsel. In that Saturn contained all of the children who delineate the power and controlling aspects of consciousness, he can be thought of as a type of consciousness that operates from a power base, full of great ideas that he himself cannot put into action: again, the wise old man, the guru of the psychoanalytic couch, the ashram, and the astrological consulted hour. What releases the children of Kronos from their predicament is insight into Kronos. Insight makes the limiting and limited flow — which is exactly what happens to Kronos at this stage in the tale. There is a particular stage in the development of consciousness that demands we relinquish power, that we stop spiritualizing and lose the battle. Insight brings us to this point, and she brings it to us in a way that forces us to throw up and throw over all that we have assimilated of the world and of ourselves. It is at this point, at our weakest, no longer nourished by what we have carefully made and contained, that we fall as Kronos. There is a limit to consciousness itself, specifically Kronian consciousness, and at this moment we fall into ourselves.

Hesiod tells us that Kronos is banished to Tartaros, and he describes this as a region bounded by a bronze fence, backed up by a triple density of night or darkness, and surrounded by a wall. Here, he adds, we find the sources and ends of both the earth and the starry heaven. Atlas stands there holding the world upon his shoulders. Tartaros, in other words, is the beginning and end of *all* things. If Tartaros were destroyed, so too would the earth and starry heaven be. The support of all that we are, the heroic Atlas, would disappear. Obviously, Tartaros — this final prison of Saturn — is a special place. It is basic to human existence.

We are also informed that both day and night spend their time there, one at a time, greeting each other as they pass over the threshhold. The stay-at-home is obligated to hold in his or her arms the brother of death, sleep. Here, then, all opposites exist and find their root and resting place. Saturn is essentially the prisoner and lord of this place. Before this prison, Hesiod continues, are to be found the halls of Hades, Master of Souls. James Hillman has emphasized the fact that the underworld is the place of soul, and that access to soul can be gained only through an experience of death at the psychological level. The importance of such death reflects mythologically from the fact that in the regions of Tartaros /Hades our soul is stable, for as Plato points out: "The souls in Hades can neither be changed nor cured of what they are."[30] These regions are the only place where I can experience soul without fluctuations brought about by the intervention of consciousness.

The movement of Kronos from the upperworld to the underworld is a movement away from the realm of conscious-making, in the direction of soul-making. To follow Kronos here is to arrive at the base of my soul. This journey can be achieved only by insighting, by an archetypal imagining that allows the unconscious easy access to consciousness. It is a way of seeing, of visioning, that our culture describes as pathological — but which we find so attractive in Eastern cultures.

The horoscope of the individual is still a way for this vision to be achieved *if* the counsellor realizes that everything in a chart need not be interpreted but rather can be experienced and imagined. This is Jung's one true way in which we can transform nature — through the experience of the image first hand. This is also what Heraclitus meant when he wrote that "those who sleep are workers and share in the activities going on in the universe,"[31] for those who sleep are nightly engaged with the images given us by the deep psyche, sent up from the realm of Kronos and Hades.

Let me conclude by saying that the danger of Kronos lies in his lending us the illusion of age-old wisdom, while at the same time imprisoning us in a wisdom that is dry and cannot see outside of itself. The beauty of Kronos, on the other hand, is that he is a God who through tribulation is capable of bringing us to a full appreciation of ourselves from the pit of the soul.

The greatest danger for astrology is to be found in the Kronian tendency to spiritualize the person — to make of his chart a thing without soul. It would be a great pity if astrology were to become just another psychology of consciousness, for it is only in astrology where we find the Classical representations of the Gods and of the soul unabashedly presented as powers residing beyond the control of ego, as mysteries whose movements and effects might be clocked and predicted, but whose ulterior motives may never be understood. To lose this sense of mystery in favor of respectable acceptance would be the final insult the modern person could offer to the archetypal ground that daily effects us. Within the context of all that has been said above, it would be the curse of Saturn accomplished.

NOTES

[1] Jung, C.G., *The Collected Works* (CW), vol. 8, par. 964, Pantheon Books, New York, 1960.

[2] Corbin, Henry, "*Mundus Imaginalis* or the Imaginary and the Imaginal," *Spring: An Annual of Archetypal Psychology and Jungian Thought*, Spring Publications, New York, 1972, p. 11.

[3] Hillman, James, "The Dream and the Underworld," *Eranos Jahrbuch 1973*, E.J. Brill, Leiden, 1975, p. 256.

[4] Jung, CW 9, i, par. 50.

[5] For further information, see my *The Game of Wizards: Psyche, Science, and Symbolism in the Occult*, Penguin Books, Baltimore, Maryland, 1975, pp. 19-74.

[6] Freud, Sigmund, "A Child is Being Beaten," in *Collected Papers*, Basic Books, New York, 1959, vol. 2, pp. 197-8.

[7] Neumann, Erich, *The Origins and History of Consciousness*, Pantheon Books, New York, 1964, p. 125.

[8] Jung, C.G., CW 14, par. 222.

[9] *ibid.*, par. 223.

[10] *ibid.*, par. 223.

[11] Stein, Murray, "The Devouring Father," in *Fathers and Mothers*, Patricia Berry, editor, Spring Publications, New York, 1973, pp. 64-74.

[12] Paracelsus, *The Hermetic and Alchemical Writings of*, Shambhala, Berkeley, 1976, vol. II, p. 285.

[13] *ibid.*, p. 309.

[14] Paracelsus, *The Secrets of Alchymy*, R. Turner, trans., London, 1656, p. 21.

[15] Jung, CW 18, par. 149ff.

[16] Hillman, James, *Re-Visioning Psychology*, Harper & Row, New York, 1975, p. x.

[17] Jung, C.G., *Two Essays on Analytical Psychology*, Meridian Books, New York, 1956, p. 225.

[18] *ibid.*, p. 227.

[19] Jung, C.G., CW 8, par. 408.

[20] Hillman, James, "An Essay on Pan," *Pan and the Nightmare, Two Essays*, Spring Publications, New York, 1972, p. xxiv.

[21] Casey, Edward S., "Toward an Archetypal Imagination," Spring Publications, New York, 1974, pp. 1-32.

[22] Jung, C.G., CW 8, par. 189.

[23]Scott, Walter, ed. and trans., *Corpus Hermeticum*, Clarendon Press, Oxford, England, vol. I, p. 221.

[24]Wilhelm, Richard & Jung, C.G., *The Secret of the Golden Flower*, Wehman Bros., New York, 1955, p. 112.

[25]Freeman, Kathleen, *The Pre-Socratic Philosophers*, Harvard University Press, Cambridge, 1966, Heraclitus fragment 77.

[26]*ibid.*, frag. 36.

[27]quoted in Lindsay, Jack, *The Origins of Alchemy in Graeco-Roman Egypt*, Barnes & Noble, Inc., New York, 1970, p. 119.

[28]quoted in Jung, C.G., CW 14, p. 335, footnote 288.

[29]*ibid.*

[30]Plato, *The Collected Dialogues of*, Hamilton & Cairns, editors, Princeton University Press, Princeton, N.J., 1973, "Gorgias," 525e.

[31]Freeman, Kathleen, *op. cit.*, frag. 75.

AN ALCHEMICAL ALLEGORY:
Notes Toward An Understanding Of Genesis

    The OED informs us that 'archaic' defines that which is "marked by the characteristics of an earlier period: old-fashioned, primitive, antiquated." One would at first be reluctant to identify oneself with anything so defined. After all, the call of the Western psyche is that of the modern, the progressive, and the futuristic. The OED also informs us that 'modern' has its roots in the Latin *modo*, 'just now' or 'of today.' Yet, it is a rare event to find a 'just now' or 'of today' with the freshness of an isolated, independent, newly created moment. 'Just nows' are more often than not experienced as the flower of the 'just before,' of the archaic, of the antiquated. When I look at others, and in society in general, I cannot help recognizing that the attitudes and lifestyles, the philosophies and political systems that affect all of us fail to meet the definition of the modern. They may appear to define my 'just now,' my 'of the moment,' but the underbelly of their appearance is archaic. When I think of democracy, I think of the Greeks; of medicine, the Arabs; astronomy, the Babylonians; computers, Leibniz and the *I Ching*; Ethics, Aristotle; and Love, Socrates. I live by virtue of the Past.

When I turn to my own soul, I find that it fits the dictionary definition of the archaic. It is then that I am truly faced with the problem of the modern, of the 'just now.' If I am the expression of the soul, if all that I am is ultimately predicated by the dynamism of this deep interior principle, where am I to find my modernity?

This flow of soul is the constant of Being, and becomes the defining property of *bios* as long as I fail to separate the two and reconnect soul with the image of *zoe*, unlimited life. *Bios* defines an eternal ground. What my liver does today, it did seven thousand years ago, and could do seven thousand years from now. As long as soul is not differentiated from *bios*, there is no 'just now' or 'of today.' What makes a thing modern is the thing's relationship to the principle of unlimited life, for only the perception of *zoe* as the wings of soul can liberate the mind and the individual from the uninterrupted flow of the past back into itself. The perception of soul as *zoe* then leads to the future. The 'just now' can come about only by a purposeful intervention, an interruption of a psychological or spiritual nature that frees soul from the known and the expected so that it might lead us deeper into what is not fated in ourselves.

What is it that is not fated? The ground of our imagination which in the past was itself the method of transformation. Thus it was that Heraclitus, pointing towards the power of the image to connect us with the unlimited, wrote "Those who sleep are workers and share in the activities going on in the universe."

The way of transformation, the creation of the now, is image and imagination. And here is the paradox: what is modern in me can become so only by virtue of my conscious involvement with the archaic—with the soul. Such an involvement must take place at several levels, however. It is not sufficient that I work on myself and nothing more. I must also work on the image and myths that have worked on me through my culture. In that way, through that kind of work, we can all hope to liberate ourselves from cultural ideas; otherwise we are imprisoned by the endless passage through one imagination to another. As Ibn 'Arabi put it, "The whole of existence is imagination within imagination, while the true being is God alone."

It is with such considerations in mind that I offer the following, a preliminary attempt to understand a myth central to the psychology of our cultural background. Some of the proposals set forth may appear blasphemous, but to me the greater blasphemy is the silence that has surrounded the questions that the myth poses.

Hermaphrodism and the Fruit of Sin

The tale of *Genesis* is too well known to be repeated in its entirety. The important features necessary for our discussion are as follows:
1. God creates Adam in His own image.
2. He forbids him to eat of the Tree of the Knowledge of Good and Evil lest he die.
3. He creates Eve from a rib in Adam's side.
4. The serpent induces Eve to eat of the Tree and convince Adam that he should also.
5. Immediately upon eating of the Tree both their eyes are opened and they perceive each other's nakedness.
6. God discovers the 'sin' and banishes the two to the desert outside of Paradise.

There are many who will insist that this is a superficial outline of a tale replete with hidden meanings, and they would be right. But none of those meanings are on the surface of the tale. It is precisely because the surface of the tale has influenced our culture that we shall ignore these imagined subtler meanings. It is sometimes necessary when discussing such material to suffer the embarrassment of naked exposition, remembering all the while that it is a natural tendency to look for the hidden while overlooking the obvious.

The first symbol to be considered is that of the hermaphroditic Adam. The hermaphrodite, in general, must be recognized as a symbolic expression of two different types of psychic orientation or consciousness, the masculine portion representing all that may be identified with the male, the feminine with all that which may be identified with the female. And here we are faced with a problem, for each culture imposes certain of its own deficiencies and expectations into the definitions of these polarities. An apparent instance of this may be found in the general attitude that the feminine is the more inferior and weaker of the two; a less apparent instance, coming from contemporary quarters where the value of the feminine is undergoing rejuvenation, is that the masculine is self-centered and tyrannical. We must in our inquiry temporarily put aside any discussion of what may or may not be the true "qualities" of the masculine and the feminine and instead address ourselves solely to the fact of their polarity. It is not our place here to discuss sexuality *per se*, but rather to discuss the symbolism of the hermaphrodite which is basically asexual.

The figure of a bi-sexual being has been traditionally employed in the language of symbolism to demarcate the beginning and end of a process. To us in the West the most familiar figure of a beginning state is the original Adam containing his wife within him. The Jewish branch of mysticism known as Kabbalism recognizes the implications of this symbolism and traditionally has taken it also to symbolize the end of their mystical quest. To their way of thinking every man is both masculine and feminine. The Sefirothic system as paradigmatic of the human body is an apt depiction of this idea. The Christian European alchemist was in basic agreement with this Kabbalistic view, with the difference that the androgynous figure standing at the end of their process was the Christ in the form of the Philosopher's Stone. What is curious is that both Judaism and Christianity begin with and accept the figure of the hermaphrodite as well but neither of them hold the figure up as symbolic of a religious life. In each instance it was necessary that the renegade factor, the mystics and philosophers working outside of the mainstream of traditional religious belief, reveal the nature of the end process in these terms. The difference between the first and second representations of the bi-sexual being represents a unity that has come about through the agency of a transformative experience— one that has caused the polarities therein to perceive one another, suffer each other's differences, and reconcile their divergent natures under the auspices of love.

The opposites in their original hermaphrodite symbolize a condition of unconsciousness wherein they reside in blissful ignorance of one another. This original status also occurs, or is implied in those world mythologies where we are told that the anthropomorphic figures of heaven and earth as father and mother existed in an undivided state; so too in mystical theologies where the polarities

An Alchemical Allegory

expressive of the human condition are illustrated as entwined or enmeshed with one another: the Kundalini entwined around the lingam in Tantric yoga and the yin and yang as exemplary of two modes of action enmeshed in the figure of the T'ai Chi of Chinese philosophy. In each instance, the implication is that the figure is either symbolic of the androgynous total unity of God, or God himself.

When the God of *Genesis* "and all the host of heaven standing beside him on his right hand and on his left" (I *Kings* 22:19) said "Let us make man in our image, after our likeness" (*Genesis* 1:26), He too created a hermaphroditic figure modeled after Himself. However, the admonition given this newborn creature not to eat of the Tree of the Knowledge of Good and Evil implies that he is not a true image. At the most, the creature's awareness is limited to a process of naming (". . . and whatever the man called every living creature, that was its name" *Genesis* 2:19) similar to that encountered in a young child.

The radical alteration of God's image by His own hand that occurs when He extracts Eve from the body of Adam represents the first act of differentiation that occurs within the infantile psyche. Here, the first step away from the unconscious hermaphrodite is taken with the appearance of two distinct units or opposites. But with this first act of differentiation a strange event occurs. The division of the figures yields a type of creature God had not anticipated. Here for the first time the *possibility* of human consciousness occurs. And that possibility comes to fruition when Eve is induced by the Serpent to eat of the Tree and then to convince Adam to follow suit.

> Then the eyes of both were opened, and they knew that they were naked, and they sewed fig leaves together and made themselves aprons. (*Genesis* 3:7)

Suddenly, for the first time since their separation out of the original hermaphrodite modelled after their Maker the two *perceive* one another. They look at each other and see each other in their nakedness; they have feeling for one another. They have become Gods in that they are capable of perceiving the opposites, and it is this ability that abruptly separates them from the lower order of creatures, that makes them not only unique, but in part divine. For the divinity of being is consciousness, and consciousness is the one sin that we all commit when we move away from the commandments of the paradisical lassitude of our unconscious natures. It is for this first act of disobedience against the thing which would keep us as children, blind to the reality that everywhere touches us, that the gates of Paradise become barred. So too in the maturing child does there come a time when the free-floating pleasures of childhood suddenly end, the young ego seemingly cast out forever into the harsh and seemingly unsupportive desert of consciousness.

But one should not read too much into the idea that consciousness is in itself divine. It is that which makes us unique in the biological order because it has allowed us to create a second Genesis, the person-made world that overlays the world of nature. In this sense it is a miraculous happening, because of all forms of consciousness on the planet it is capable of concretizing the images that from time to time arise within us into created forms. So one might easily mistake the creative ability of human consciousness as divine, turning the diminutive ego into a hubristic monarch. What is divine in human consciousness, *per se*, is its ability to engage in soul-making activity as well as world-making. As James Hillman puts it, "The human adventure is wandering through the vale of the world for the sake of making soul. Our life is psychological, and the purpose of life is to make psyche of it, to find connections between life and soul."[1] For this we, both as men and women, need the Eve in us.

The harshness of the young ego's first encounter with all that exists outside of the paradisical unconscious is nowhere better illustrated than in the Apocryphal *Book of Adam and Eve* where we are told of Adam's several attempts at suicide immediately upon being cast out of Eden. Adam's predicament is a simple one: he is suddenly subject to the hardships of being-in-the-world, witness to the burden of consciousness that the ego must take up to accomplish successfully the transition from the paradise of a childhood free of conflict to the reality of the opposites of which our world appears to be composed. It is this willingness to take upon oneself the conflict of the opposites that exist beyond the gates of Paradise that gives birth to the transformative experience of suffering; it is this painful paradox to which the serpent awakens the first couple.

What we might have in the figure of Adam is a picture of the germinal ego coming into being in the pleroma of the unconscious.

That the Adam of Paradise represents what will become an important aspect of ego is implied in the fact that he is made in the image of God, and that as God rules over the paradise of the unconscious, Adam too will one day rule over the desert of consciousness existing beyond the Gates of Paradise. In short, the ego that rules consciousness is but the image of God, or the Self, that rules our unconscious.[2] The differentiation of this ego begins while it is still within the gates of the unconscious and is symbolized by the extraction of the feminine principle which (we are told) is of the essence of bone. That is, the feminine on the way to becoming has its origin in a thing many religions symbolically identify as eternal and divine. Even in our culture the skeleton, which alone remains after death, is symbolic of the barrier between the transpersonal and the mundane, between being and non-being. Both primitive and more advanced cultures employ different portions of the skeleton as *mana* objects, treating them as they would divinity itself. In addition, this feminine figure is taken from that portion of Adam's body closest to the heart — the place traditionally identified with emotion and intuitive knowledge. Eve is a portion of what is at once hidden but supportive, eternal and divine, wisdom-inducing and passionate; she symbolizes a component of our being that is both immortal and human; that mediates between being and non-being: the soul.

Universally it is the soul's function to mediate between the human world and the divine; she is often described as the bearer of messages in the form of dreams and visions — in other words, she operates through the realm of images. It is in this sense that the soul might be thought of as that which mediates between consciousness and the unconscious. It is because of the inquisitiveness of this soul principle that consciousness is won from the unconscious, that it is Eve who leads Adam to the fruit of the Tree. This too, traditionally, is a function of the soul: to inform, to direct, to guide, and to cause enlightenment. With this act of defiance the true separation from the unconscious takes place. The ego becomes locked out of Paradise, the soul going with it into the desert, her connectedness to the divine serving as the only link between the transpersonal and the mundane. The idea of the feminine soul exiled from the divine and trapped on earth is also a common theme in mythology and world religion.

Between the initial state of the hermaphrodite symbolic of the unconscious union of the opposites and the final state of the androgyne symbolic of the marriage of all opposites in consciousness, there then appear the stages of life comprised of the conflict of the opposites.

The Wisdom of the Serpent

"Now the serpent was more subtle than any other wild creature that the Lord God had made." (*Genesis* 3:25). That the serpent is "more subtle" is a major understatement. Here was the sole non-human creature in the Garden not only capable of speech, but of also knowing that God was lying to Adam when He told him that the fruit of the tree would cause death. The serpent tells Eve she need not fear the tree:

> You will not die. For God knows that when you eat of it your eyes will be opened and you will be like God, knowing Good and Evil.

The serpent is a cold-blooded creature who in at least one system of transformation (Kundalini yoga) has been identified with the sympathetic nervous system; that is, with the so-called autonomous portion of our being. Because the serpent symbolizes transformation through its activity of skin-shedding, and because it knows the true results when the fruit of the Tree of Knowledge of Good and Evil is eaten, we must assume that it represents yet another form of consciousness. Considering the serpent and his relation to the first couple, it obviously represents the consciousness of the psychic system that comes into being when the human organism becomes a reality. It is, in other words, the inborn instinctual wisdom that God had not reckoned on, the spirit in nature that complements the spirit of God hovering above the waters of Creation. In the same manner that God is complemented by the figure of Adam, so is the spirit of God complemented by the spirit in nature. This is the core of our uniqueness. We contain a spirit that is diametrically opposed to the Spirit of God who originally desired the perfection and stability of a Paradise. The spirit of nature, on the other hand, demands imperfection and change, for without these two states the need for and experience of transformation does not occur. This is something that God Himself had no knowledge of originally: transformation. He was complete in

Himself, without imperfection. The serpent in psychological terms may be thought of as the cold-blooded range of instincts through which we experience transformation. Thus transformation comes to us through the instinctual range of our experience, through the first-hand experience of our autonomous nature.

All of which leads us to an important question: What is the serpent in relation to God? How is it that of all the creatures in the Garden it alone was capable of knowing God's most secret thoughts; what is it about this creature that allows it to know the true secret of the Tree, that allows it to know what even God Himself appears to be ignorant of — that the creature/Eve carries within her the seed of consciousness in the form of curiosity and that questions about the unknown are a temptation to her? Here we are obviously faced with a consciousness equal to God's in that it not only knows the past, the true value of the Tree, the psychic disposition of Eve, but also has some inkling of the potentialities inherent in the entire situation. We can only conclude from these facts that the serpent is symbolic of an aspect of God Himself, that its almost God-like consciousness is just that — a split-off portion of God's psyche.

The Dream of God

Now we must consider the phenomenon of Genesis from God's viewpoint, investigating the possible reasons for His committing Himself to the act. Throughout *Genesis,* up to the creation of the androgynous Adam, God goes about the entire matter of Creation in a rather straight-forward manner. We gain little insight into His psychology or His feelings until the day when He says to Himself:

> It is not good that the man should be alone; I will make him a helper fit for him. (*Genesis* 2:18)

In this statement we have a clue to why the project of Creation was ever undertaken, for God's ability to empathize with another's loneliness could only have grown out of a first-hand experience. There are a number of world mythologies that tell us the Creation of the universe arose from the Creator's experience of loneliness and the ensuing desire to create something that he could relate to. A vintage example is given us in the Winnebago Creation myth.

What it was our father lay on when he came to consciousness we do not know. . . He began to think of what he should do and finally began to cry. . . He said, "As things are just as I wish them I shall make one being like myself." So he took a piece of earth and made it like himself. Then he talked to what he had created but it did not answer. He looked upon it and he saw that it had no mind or thought. So he made a mind for it. Again he talked to it, but it did not answer. . . So he looked upon it again and saw that it had no soul. So he made it a soul. He talked to it again and it very nearly said something. But it did not make itself intelligible. So Earthmaker breathed into its mouth and talked to it and it answered.[3]

Again, in the *Satapatha Brahmana* we are told that the soul of the universe, Purusha, was alone. Hence,

He did not enjoy happiness. He desired a second. He caused this same self to fall asunder into two parts. Thence there arose a husband and wife. From them men were born.[4]

The striking similarity between the Winnebago tale and *Genesis*, right down to the creation of an Eve-soul for the creature and the imparting of breath by Earthmaker to animate his creature is apparent. Our example from Hindu mythology also complements *Genesis* in that the Creator himself is a hermaphroditic creature whose division gives birth to the first couple. In *Genesis*, God does not perform this operation on Himself but instead creates a creature in His own image in much the same manner that the Winnebago God does. In both instances, as in others too long to relate here, the creation begins because of God's experience of loneliness. In our Western tale, God does not start straight off with the creation of a divine couple but, as earlier in the Winnebago tale, sets about the creation of the world proper. The experience of loneliness, these tales appear to be telling us, can be a creative experience if handled properly. That is, the experience if turned inwards unites one with unknown aspects of one's own personality—in this instance, one's creative abilities. Ultimately, loneliness is something or someone representative or symbolic of an interior component of ourselves that longs to be united with us, or that we long to be united with. Expressed psychologically, this yearning is for something that is not known to us consciously, that is hidden deep within our souls. We humans are afforded opportunities to gain access to the hidden portions of our-that appear in either dreams, forth the imaginative faculty tute disciplined meditational ... that allows the unconscious to display itself during the waking state. Jung called this particular method (active imagination) a short-cut to the unconscious, for it allows inner being immediate access to consciousness, and *vice versa*.

Because in these versions the act of Creation grows out of a conscious decision on the part of God ("Let us make . . ."), we would here suggest that the Creation took place through an experiment in imagination. In an attempt to discover the hidden aspect of Himself with which He wished to be united, God allowed His unconscious to create an image of the material attempting to come into the light of consciousness. In much the same manner that the unconscious in human beings creates dreams reflective of our hidden nature, so too did God spin out of His unconscious that aspect of His hidden nature with which He was not reconciled. Whereas our unconscious lives are ephemeral and without material substance, His unconscious life took on substance. His images were to have as much life as the images we find in our dreams; His images were to live themselves forward regardless of His commandments in much the same manner that the process of our unconscious lives live themselves forward regardless of our conscious and rational commands. The creation of a creature in His own image constituted an attempt at introspection, an attempt to "get a look" at Himself, as it were. The androgynous Adam would therefore be symbolic of the unknown and hidden value that was attempting to become united with His consciousness. In other words, Adam symbolized the proverbial fly in the ointment, the unknown portion of God's psyche that constituted His blind spot.

The figure of Adam symbolizes the problem concealed in God's psyche; humanity represents the psychological process that God undergoes by committing Himself to an act of creative imagination. The pain and conflict that we undergo in our attempts at selfawareness are but symbolic of the same process God undergoes through the history of the human race. We are the conflict, the pain, the confusion of His own transformation. History is God's self-analysis. We are His dream over which He has as little control as we do ours. For us to affect the nature of our dream lives creatively and positively we must first arrive at a proper conscious standpoint in our relationship with the unconscious. So too, we assume, must God act toward his "unconscious," the sphere of which is the created world, if He is to realize the dark and unknown aspect of his own personality symbolized by the serpent. This now brings us to the question of what God might have been unconscious of to begin with.

The Serpent on the Cross

The experience of loneliness, the yearning for the unknown and unseen within us, the thing scratching at our dreams, can, if not properly attended to, lead us into states of inexplicable rage. Invariably, one ends up vacillating between the experience of extreme emotion and boredom. As Paul Tillich once surmised, boredom is rage spread thin. The phenomenon of rage presents us with a peculiar ambiguity. On the one hand, a person overcome with rage usually appears to be acting out of a passionate emotion, in the "heat of anger" as it is usually referred to. On the other hand the results of such a state are actually unfeeling acts. Hidden within this so-called heat of anger is a cold-blooded instinctual response to situations that the individual for some reason or other finds untenable. One aspect of the symbolism of the serpent in the tale of *Genesis* is just this type of cold-bloodedness. In the light of the frequent outbursts of rage that the *Old Testament* God often displays, we would suggest here that the serpent (which we have described as a split-off portion of God's psyche) symbolizes the cold-blooded and instinctual side of God's unrealized difficulty. The fact that God is not aware of the knowledge that the serpent contains, the fact that he overlooks its presence in the Garden of his imagination, indicates that He is not only blind to this rage, but that He has actually repressed it out of sight. In that the serpent is also symbolic of transformative powers and consciousness; the secret of God's problem is to be discovered in the very thing that He rejects. However, rage and cold-bloodedness, loneliness and boredom are only symptoms. The serpent is but the energic principle of the unrealized problem symbolized by the hermaphroditic Adam. The problem is to be found in God's unity.

What the image of Himself reveals to God is the fact that the unity He represents is composed of opposites. Because God, not only in our tradition but in every tradition known to us, is defined as a unity of opposites, the one thing that He cannot know of is the experience of the opposites in a divided state. God has the *knowledge* of the opposites, but not the *experience* of their effect. He has experienced only their peaceful unity. The knowledge that He has of them constitutes a philosophical assumption. In order to experience the true effect of the opposites He must first divide them. This is the nature of God's blind spot in *Genesis*, the source of his rage in the *Old Testament* — this little piece of unconsciousness concerning an aspect of His psyche of which He has had no experience.

So, the events of *Genesis*, from the beginning up to the expulsion from Eden, are symbolized throughout by division. With the division of the androgynous Adam into male and female the process of self-awareness begins. However, as is more often than not the case, this first attempt to take a look at Himself fails, for He assumes (as we also so often do) that He knows exactly what He looks like, knows without a doubt all the components of His personality. Adam, however, is a pure intellectual construction, for he is made up of those things that God chooses as relevant for his creation. The active and motivating principles of His problem, the energy necessary for transformation symbolized by the serpent, is repressed, overlooked, lurking in the Garden's shadows. Adam as symbolic of God's problem is an intellectualization similar to those lists we often compose as illustrative of our good and bad qualities. God does not really want to consider the moral problems posed by His knowledge of Good and Evil, hence He leaves those qualities out of the image He would employ as an introspective aid. But the unconscious will not allow Him to escape the issue. The repressed value intrudes itself and sets up a situation in which the moral issue He does not want to consider is presented to Him in a symbolic play. It shows Him that the repressed value contains transformative energies and a consciousness of its own; that to achieve consciousness and discover the nature of one's own inferiority it is at times necessary to go against one's own ego-dominated commandments. In this regard, the serpent symbolizes the innate wisdom of the instinctual portion of the psyche to heal and transform itself. It attempts to reveal this fact to God, but instead of pausing long enough to consider that the mishap came about because of an error in His judgement, He elects to pass the blame on. The suffering that would have arisen by His wrestling with the problems in the issue of Good and Evil is instead heaped on the shoulders of His creation. In other words, He represses the problem even further through projection.

What the serpent attempted to show God on the stage of Paradise was that transformation can be experienced only by a willingness to take on the suffering implicit in any act of becoming consciouss; that to gain access to an unrealized portion of His own being, God would have to experience the conflict of the opposites at first hand. To achieve this He would have to commit Himself totally to the experiment. The task would have been easier if He had dealt with it within the confines of His carefully constructed vessel called Paradise. Having failed in that experiment, He would have to follow the lead that the psyche imposed on Him. He would have to experience the conflict *in* the world, which in His reality meant that he would have to make a total descent into His unconscious. In short, He would have to become mortal in the figure of the Christ in order to experience the conflict peculiar to humanity. It would only be there, on the Cross, in that mass of nerve and muscle, that God could experience what was unknown to Him: the conflict inherent in the disunity that expresses itself in suffering. It was only in this manner that the symptoms of His unconsciousness could be transformed. It was there where the serpent of His psyche would in time be experienced firsthand by that manifestation of Himself in the form of the Christ who would himself say, during a discussion on the necessity of being reborn:

> And as Moses lifted up the serpent in the wilderness, so must the Son of man be lifted up, that whoever believes in him may have eternal life. (*John* 3:14,15)

And in such a manner was God eventually to resolve his psychic difficulty. From a wrathful, vengeful, and unpredictable despot He was transformed into a God of Love through the agency of our humanity. It is through this act of transformation that the androgyne appears in the person of Christ who by his traditional identification with the Second Adam becomes associated with the bi-sexual figure which began the process.

The Christ therefore symbolized the suffering inherent in the fusion of the divine with the human portions of our psyches. That is, it is at that point where we suffer the greatest anguish in the desert of this world to which we have been exiled that we may know we are contributing to the self-realization of God Himself. It is only during such moments in the Work that we may fully know we are in the presence of the archetypal.

And in all this there is concealed the meaning of the statement that the Stone is the Christ and that the stages of the Work are revealed to us in the seven days of Creation. By this it is to be understood that God's task was that of separating the opposites so that He could experience their differences: and that our task is that of uniting the opposites so that we might have the knowledge of their unity, which is God.

This is the meaning of the marriage of the sun and moon, of the solar and lunar consciousness we have been allotted, and without whose union we deny God the experience of Himself.

NOTES

[1] *Re-Visioning Psychology*, James Hillman, Harper & Row Publishers, New York, 1975, p. ix.

[2] *vide*, C.G. Jung, "The ego . . . is a relatively constant personification of the unconscious . . ." CW 14, p. 107.

[3] quoted in *From Primitives to Zen*, Mircea Eliade, Harper & Row, New York, 1967, pp. 83-4.

[4] *ibid.*, p. 151.

WOMAN, THE FEMININE, AND ALCHEMY

In truth, what follows are considerations on the nature of man, specifically his unconscious condition as expressed in his religious and mystical experience. In all aspects of this experience we find a theory of woman which is at first sight romantic, but on closer inspection demeaning. I bring these issues up in the manner of a suggestion—that as we in the secular world now begin the business of re-defining the roles of men and women, we not lose sight of the fact that practically all of our mystical traditions are the creations of men and that in these systems there may lie concealed, in poetic garb, those same insinuations of masculine superiority that we now discover in the mundane sphere.

All of this would point to the idea that many aspects of our mystical and religious traditions must be reconsidered if they are to be married to reality—and married they must be if we are to ever become one with that which we call God.

I for one do not find it possible to speak *to* woman of either her psychology or her present condition. At most, I may speak of my relationship to the feminine, and from there the nature of my awareness of Woman as an Other. And here is the crux of the problem. Each of us, men and women alike, are contained units, monads of pure energy or "windowless beings" as Leibniz put it. Much in our relationships is based upon assumption and phantasy. We came together in a seeming unity of understanding based on shared experiences in which we find a similarity of response. Ultimately, all of our feelings towards one another are based on an imaginal realm of hazy similitude, or at least the feeling of conviction that "we know" what the other is feeling, has felt, is experiencing. The closer we are in terms of sex, background, education, religion, etc., the less pronounced is the effect of this imaginal realm. But when we are confronted with an Other, one whose biological structure is different from ours, the imaginal quality of the relationship becomes heightened and the vacuum of our ignorance becomes a vessel for the imperceptible—for the soul.

I do not mean to imply that the experience of those aspects of soul that are felt as personal can only be known in love relationships between members of the opposite sex. I make reference to the image of the couple as a team in this essay solely because it appears often in alchemy, the implication being that the work is one concerned with the oppositional and distinctively different qualities of certain psychic realities. At the same time, however, while the soul can be experienced through a deep encounter with an idea, a condition, a work, it is doubtful that a real engagement can occur without a considerable measure of loving.

The feeling of "knowing the Other," the intensity of the knowledge of the Other "body and soul" should not be set aside as mere illusion, for it is the very thing that bonds humankind together. This feeling of "knowing," the intimacy of a shared experience, is a phenomenon of love or Eros. Because I speak here of Eros as a Power, a dynamic energy of an archetypal nature, a God in the classical sense, its intimacy should be understood as a total receptiveness to and common containment in the God Himself. This, essentially, is what being *in* love means.

The alchemists knew that this imperceptible quantity is the thing called forth in an encounter with an Other, with either the wife as "fellow worker," or the image of the female as counterpart. In either case, what we are talking about is the image of the soul and the idea that one's relationship with that image will always be a determining factor in any real encounter with others. This is all the more reason why it is imperative at this juncture in history to review the image of soul in alchemical, religious, and mythological thought. This must be done to determine whether the earlier views are commensurate with the insights of our twentieth-century experience or were from the outset generalizations founded on a basic misunderstanding of the nature of the opposites.

In the long run it is only through an acknowledgement of our interiority that we may come to see the Other as a person and not as a fragment of our imprisoned souls projected upon them. Without such an acknowledgement all forms of soul-work must be considered worthless.

> The union of the sexes is four-membered rather than two-membered: it always means the complex union of the male element of the one with the female element of the other, and of the female element of the first with the male element of the second. The mystical life of the androgyne is realized not in one bisexual being but rather in the quadripartite union of two beings. (Nicholas Berdyaev)

There appears to be a universal law, unfortunate in its implications, which states that wherever you find a religious or mystical system that exalts the feminine, making of it a divine attribute through which salvation may be known, in the society where that view is furthered you will find a proportionate disregard of woman as social being. One can almost postulate a law of compensation. From the Virgin Mary to Shakti to Yin and to the Shekhinah of Kabbalistic doctrine, the case holds true. Woman as a spiritual factor is the desired, but woman as an existent in her own right is exemplary of a downfallen clod of earth.

The first point in fact is the Kabbalistic doctrine that tells us that the feminine portion of God, the Shekhinah, is in exile in the world. In the configuration known as the Sefirothic Tree of Life we find a fourfold division known as the Four World system. The doctrine of this system will be known to most of my readers. For those who are not familiar with it let them know that I am here concerned only with the problems presented by the fourth world, that associated with this world, our earth.

In the Sefirothic system the fourth world is identified with the sefirah Malkuth, The Kingdom, which is again symbolic of our place of existence. This sefirah Malkuth *is* the Shekhinah, the exiled feminine portion of God that longs to be united with Him — and with good reason, for she represents the grossest part of creation in which reside the evil spirits known as the *kellipoth*.

To make matters worse, the triad of the Kabbalistic soul, which is also described as feminine, is thought of as manifesting itself along the course of the first three worlds. That is, the first and purest portion of the soul is associated with the sefirah Kether, that sefirah furthest removed from mankind. The second portion of the soul, that which is synonymous with the moral element of God, is identified with the sefirah Tifereth which unites the Sefiroth of the second world. Lastly, the third division of the soul, that portion which is identified with the animal life and desires and unites the Sefiroth of the third world, is located in the sefirah Yesod, the sefirah symbolic of the male and female genitals. The fourth world, however, that which *is* the feminine, the Shekhinah, God's helpmate and love, *has no share of the soul.* It is soulless.

Add to this the disconcerting fact that the salvation of mankind, the restitution of the divine portion of God to God, was considered by both the Rabbinic and Kabbalistic tradition to be the work and concern of men, a divine job in which woman as social being played no role other than that of model of the catastrophe known as the Fall, and you have a pretty good picture of the attitude towards woman in that mystical setting.

Turning to the Orient we find matters just as bad, with yin and yang representative of woman and man respectively. The yang is defined as that which is light and positive, the yin as that which is dark and negative. For a Taoist monk to achieve the balance of these opposites within himself, to equilibriate his over-plus of innate yang, he must acquire a proportionate amount of yin. This is accomplished through sexual intercourse with as many "holy" women as possible in succession without achieving ejaculation until the end of his adventure. When that moment finally does occur the practitioner must perform "retention of seed," during which time it is imagined that the semen is channelled up through the spine, the end-result being the birth of the inner-man. No mention is ever made of the woman's development in this process outside of the fact that she is "honoured."

The social position of women in ancient China is too well-known to be discussed here, but the extent to which this mystical doctrine of the opposites was taken may be seen in the following quote from a work entitled *Nu-chieh* (*The Ideal Woman*):

> The sexual union depends on Yang's ability to dominate and guide, and Yin's willingness to follow and obey. Man is wonderful for his strength, woman for her simple submissiveness . . . In the bedchamber the woman must discourage excess by her restraint, not by opposing Yang, but by transforming her own wish for "fire inside the Jade Pavilion" (orgasm) into transcendental thoughts. Excess of *Clouds and Rain* (sexual intercourse) will lead to moral depravity and finally to use of lewd words. Such a state can only result in the calamity of wifely disrespect for her master . . . A woman must be chaste and respectful, choose her words carefully, never show distress, avoid laughter or jestful behavior, refrain from peeping from windows and mixing with crowds. If she is at all times as discrete as a shadow or an echo, who can find fault with such a woman?

A good example of the Hindu attitude is to be found in the Tantric text *Kama-Kala-Vilasa* where we find a myth of the Creation. There we are told that the Great Lord Shiva, discovering that he was alone in the universe, spun out of his loneliness Desire in the shape of the Divine Feminine, his Shakti. No sooner did she see and realize his beauty when there arose in her a desire for him to experience his magnificence. To this end she transformed herself into "The Pure Mirror in which Shiva experiences Himself." Again, in an attempt to express her awe and love for Him, Shakti then went on to create out of her own body the manifest worlds of substance and sensation, the lowest and grossest being our world with which she becomes identified. All of this is rather interesting when one considers that the yogin's goal is disengagement from the world in his union with a masculine God.

And then, finally, there is our own tale of Creation where woman is created not in her own right but as a smaller portion of man. In Hebrew the word for "a woman" is *ishshah*, which is defined as a *creature* having the general appearance of a man, differing only in sex. The selection of the name *Chavvah* (Eve) is also interesting in that the Hebrew *Chavvah* is curiously reminiscent of the word for "beast," *Chayyah*.

In all of the above examples we find the feminine associated with the damned earth which is in turn the harbor of evils and the prison of the feminine. In every instance it is implied that woman or the feminine is, if not of lesser origin, certainly of a lesser state of being. The only saving feature throughout is the implication that it is necessary that the feminine be re-united with the divine. There is an urgency to this idea. There is something within the soul that is infinitely wiser than the machinery of our intellects, something which knows that things have gone amiss and that a general state of restitution is imperative.

> And I find more bitter than death the woman, whose heart is snares and nets, and her hands as bands: who so pleaseth God shall escape from her; but the sinner shall be taken by her. (*Ecclesiastes* 7:26)

> Let the woman learn in silence with all subjection. But I suffer not a woman to teach nor to usurp authority over the man, but to be in silence. For Adam was first formed, then Eve. And Adam was not deceived, but the woman being deceived was in the transgression. Notwithstanding she shall be saved in childbearing, if they continue in faith and charity and holiness with sobriety. (*I Timothy* 2:11-15)

> And if they will learn anything, let them ask their husbands at home: for it is a shame for them to speak in church. (*I Corinthians* 14:35)

What all of these traditions point to is a deficiency, a hole in the pleroma of our being that has so long been ignored that now the soul announces the problem in the most secret of our palaces — our bedrooms and our sexual instincts. This deficiency has gone so long unnoticed, even though our myths and our religions are replete with insinuation of its existence, that it now attacks us directly in the form of sexual and psychological problems, in those breakdowns of spirit we term impotence and frigidity.

*   *   *

"You will never arrive at any perfection unless Sol and Luna be united into one body."
—Laurentius Ventura

*   *   *

In every instance, the feminine is described as that which is debased, uncomely, and weak. This then is the lot of our humanity: to suffer the rejected portion of our souls. Psychology would step in here and call those portions repressed, but they are more than repressed, for the term implies that they were once known to us and purposively cast out of our lives. Nothing could be further from the truth. The condition described in these texts is a given. Thus, what alone can lead me towards my own salvation is the very thing that most naturally repels me. The alchemists were aware of this state of affairs when they wrote that the true gold is to be found in the filth by the wayside, in that which has been discarded. As they used to say, it is all around us, before our eyes, in the world. It is the archetype of the feminine: Mother-nature, sister-soul, wife-companion. It is also the archetype of matter, of stuff that makes things real. That myths inform us the feminine is matter itself implies that everything that becomes *a* matter, everything that has or gives substance to our lives must be archetypally feminine. If there is any one definition of the feminine here, it is that the feminine as matter defines any situation in which an issue having to do with one's basic and simple existence comes to the fore. We might add that issues bearing strong emotional difficulties, of a type one would prefer to reject out of hand, by corresponding with the archetypal figure of the rejected feminine also define the most important aspect of the feminine.

Whatever I ultimately define as my world, the person-created value systems that hold together my way of being in the world, that give meaning and support to my life, there is where the feminine is. She is to be found in the particulars of a life, in the foundation of any temple I might create. She is the symptom of my being, the thing that connects me to reality in a most painful way, that turns me away from the heights of conscious fabrications towards the depths of what has been given me as myself. What the feminine suffers in myth is essentially what I suffer in the myth of myself, for the feminine is not some mythological abstract reality — it is a portion of myself that it tightly knit to life, if not life itself.

In all of the myths referred to the world of humanity comes into existence *because* of her exile, her fall, the losing of her way. My humanity, everything that I define as human, ultimately has its origin in the archetypal condition of the feminine so described. If she is orphaned, I am orphaned, and if she is lost then so too am I. Wherever I fall, become lost or exiled, there I am *in* soul. And if she is also described as the body — which she is — then my most intimate connection to her will be through my body. But, again, it will be through all of these perceptions of body as base, not to be discussed, hidden away from dining-room conversations. Where my body breaks down, where my body demands of me what I would not give it, where my body embarrasses or repels me, there is the dark one of Solomon.

The depreciation of the feminine, and hence of women, since the beginnings of the Classical Period, reveals the existence of an archetype of inferiority. That is, there is in the psyche of mankind *and* womankind an idea of something inferior, dark, weak, exiled and soulless. This archetypal structure at some point in our development became projected out into the world on to women and all which is defined as feminine. It points to the existence of a split in our being that has been instrumental in the creation of institutions wherein the female and the feminine have been placed in a subordinate position. If one moves backwards into the psyche to discover the root of this attitude, what one finds is an attitude towards soul, towards the feminine aspect of the Divine. The exile of the feminine in matter as imagined by the alchemists, the personification of the feminine as earth, was considered correctly by them to signify the exile of Soul from its place in the world of being.

The fear of the feminine in the world and in ourselves is exemplary of our attitude towards that out of which it has arisen — the sea of the unconscious which even when it was "discovered" by Freud was thought of as nothing more than a garbage heap of repressions. That the earth was at one and the same time a synonym for the human body and for the feminine indicates that the alchemists understood that the problem was one of redeeming what is "feminine" in ourselves.

*   *   *

> When the period was completed, the bond by which all things were held together was loosed, by God's design; all living creatures, having till then been bisexual, were parted asunder, and man with the rest; and so there came to be males on the one part, and likewise females on the other part. (*The Poimandres of Hermes Trismegistus*, Book I, 19)

*   *   *

Spirit is, with very few exceptions, not only thought of as masculine, but as volatile and uncontained, free-ranging. Soul, on the other hand, is invariably thought of as feminine, imprisoned contained, and dedicated to nothing but union with the masculine thought of in the singular sense. In other words, Spirit is an undiscriminating and free-wheeling potency, whereas Soul is a highly discriminating and limited potential.

Traditional mythologies point to this biased fact time and again, and should be thought of as attempts to show us our condition so that we might learn where the alchemical work is to be performed, where it is that we may come into contact with what we are. The dichotomy presented to us in these tales points not to what should be used to define our social and personal relationships, but rather what defines our initial relationship to ourselves —the so-called *natural* man or woman, if you would. The dichotomy points to the split within each of us, and the employment of sexual imagery to emphasize the differences and difficulties between these polarities is an attempt to show us that the differences are basic, natural, and in the end define our humanity. But the humanity they point to is not the anthropological, the sociological, or the statistical. It is *my* humanity; the male and female of me and in me, the Adam and Eve wandering through the world on a daily basis, seeking relief from what I am.

To derive from this the idea that we are in need of transformation is to evade the issue. Transformation implies a change from bad to better, a movement away from the difficult to the manageable or sublime. To seek transformation of the feminine is to deny its reality as an archetypal given. To say the feminine is in a state of damnation and filth that must become glorified and cleansed is to deny the feminine. And yet we have made a cult of transformation. Spiritual, religious, and psychological programs all demand that we transform ourselves. And the demands that these systems place upon us is one that would have us reject the basic nature of the feminine and soul. To become better, I must reject what I am for what I should be. Invariably, what I should be is also what everyone else should be as well. The call for transformation, therefore, especially in the twentieth century, is but a call to the common, to the equal, and to the acceptable. It is the religion of a spiritual democracy that assumes all parts of myself are equal in the eyes of God. But a nightly appraisal of myself alerts me to the fact that there is much in me that is not equal. My desires and my limitations are at variance with one another. And yet simply to demand that I reduce my desires to the tight fit of my limitations would be to take away the enthusiasms natural to life — to give in and give up.

The systems of transformation that travel in magical mystery show style from one part of this country to another all at some point or another inform us that to become whole we must struggle against being ourselves. There is something wrong with this attitude, for by refusing to accept the infirmities that define us, we also refuse the soul.

If not transformation, what then? Are we simply to be and nothing more? Are we simply to exist like the flowers and the birds? I think not. This too is yet another system of transformation: our mis-reading of the Taoist "not doing." The assumption behind such a call is that everything that is in or of Nature is good and all we need do is become one with Nature. But it is curious that what is murderous, bestial, sick, dying or dead in nature never enters into the picture of this spiritual program either. Only what is beautiful and without conflict is natural. So, this is no way of depth for us either.

Karl Kerenyi has alerted us to the idea that a symbol "is the visible sign of an invisible order . . . a transparent part of the world," to be seen through.[1] And he refers us to the world as the source of symbol, not the other way around. We generally tend to think of the symbol as something other than ourselves, above or beyond us. But what if situations and realities so commonplace as to be overlooked are themselves the symbols of what Kerenyi calls an invisible order. It is not the invisible order that is symbolic, it is the visible order. And this latter order is simply the surface of a happening that *is* of itself and nothing more. It has no meaning in the psychological or hermeneutic sense but is rather a statement of archetypal fact. If so, then I would have no right to take my broken arm as an omen that something should be transformed. My condition *has already been transformed.* What I am being called upon to do at that moment is to see through experience to the archetypal lineaments of that fact. James Hillman has defined this first stage in seeing through as "a process of interiorizing,"[2] and obviously what we need for it is another set of eyes to see what is not immediately transparent.

So it is not a matter of my transforming what I am or what has become of me as much as it is a matter of my immersion in what I am to the fullest. And if this should pain me, constrict me, bind me then that is the meaning for it aptly describes the mythological experience of the soul and is a way into my soul. The meaning is the experience of myself and nothing more — but I must also be constantly aware that the "myself" I speak of is but a symbol of an invisible order. What mythology describes as the feminine must be seen through. We must reconsider many so-called spiritual truths by virtue of the fact that they may have in many instances been restated, molded, and modified by the existing social *mores* at that time when they became manifest.

In the puberty rites of male-societies the initiate is forced to cut himself off from the feminine sharply and distinctively (from the mother in particular), by acts of heroism that demand he go against his instinctual nature. It is not so much that the initiate is asked to separate himself from his mother as much as it is that he is called upon to free himself from what she symbolizes — the maternal aspects of the instincts and the deep unconscious. When functioning normally, the instincts "take care" of us — tell us when we need food, when we should advance, when we should flee, fight, befriend, etc. I understand this maternal realm to symbolize the unconscious upon which the individual is initially dependent, moved by impulses rather than by decisive and willed actions.

During the time when we are cared for by the instinctual realm, during childhood, practically any response or activity is allowed us by society. When we leave the realm of the maternal, however, we are expected to work against nature. During a man's initiation, for instance, he is not allowed to retreat, flinch, or complain of the pain inflicted upon him in any manner. In all such initiations the initiate must remain still, receiving the most painful treatment without a word or sign of discomfort. In some societies such reactions bring instant death. What is demanded is that one become independent of the maternal realm of his own being, that one through decisive action overcome instinctual response.

In an Hungarian fairy tale called *The Glass Axe* we are told the story of a Queen who on her deathbed commands her husband to,

> Never let the child [her son] put his feet on the ground, for as soon as he does so he will fall into the power of a Wicked Fairy, who will do him much harm.

As the boy grows he is carried on litters, wheeled about in chairs, and finally given a horse which he must always ride. While hunting one day he falls from his horse and touches the ground at which time, "A whole new world stretched out before him." He is then given a task by the Wicked Fairy with the warning that should be encounter a black girl in the woods he is not to speak to her on pain of death. Of course, he meets the girl and does speak with her only to discover that she is the enchanted daughter of the Wicked Fairy. To make a long story short, she promises to aid him in his tasks, one of them being the murder of the Wicked Fairy herself. With the aid of the black girl the day is won and they are wed to live happily ever after.

In this tale we find the Prince protected by the queenly aspects of the feminine, those that are removed from the basics of everyday life, ensconced in the castle heights, maternal in its protection. Much of our present involvement in the idea of the feminine and the need to reconcile ourselves with it focuses on this queenly dimension. The modern adoration of the feminine is an adoration of the feminine removed from us. It is the spiritual but distant protector capable of caring for us even in death. Whether we call this type of femininity the anima, shakti, or the Virgin Mary we cannot escape the fact that she does not allow us to come into contact with the immediate ground of our world. If anything, she encourages us to be carried about in spiritual smugness. We write papers and give lectures on the beauty of the feminine, the conjunction with the feminine, the reconciliation with the masculine portion of our psyches with the feminine — all the while refusing to see that what we applaud is not soul, but Mother. We are protected at every turning by our phantasy of the feminine as something purely pleasant and complementary.

What is it that this Queen would protect us from? From the earth, the dirt of our commonality, the dark and damned connection to soul. And the tale tells us, quite simply, that in order to come into contact with this reality one must literally fall off of one's high horse. Only then does a new world open to us. The darkness of the exiled feminine approaches us so that we can truly marry. One need only refer to the Song of Solomon to discover the significance of the maiden who is "black but comely." And it is here that our comments in "Paracelsus and the Wound" regarding our disregard of the body particularly apply.

The contrast between fairytales featuring issues central to the male psyche and those concentrating on female issues is marked. In the latter, the woman is either possessed or in a state of imprisonment during the greater part of her experience. She is either asleep or entranced, transformed into a small helpless creature or dwelling in a class or position beneath her station. She is, as our brief survey of creation myths revealed, trapped, exiled, and helpless. In every instance her life is in danger and can be saved only through the agency of the masculine, and then only through love. But the most significant clue is that the masculine himself is also in a helpless state, as in the Polish fairytale *The Crow*.

There we are told of the youngest of three Princesses who one day comes upon a torn and bleeding black crow that claims he is an enchanted Prince. He tells her that if she wished, she could save him on the condition that she "say good-bye to all of your own people and come and be my constant companion in this ruined castle. There is one habitable room in it, in which there is a golden bed . . . You will have to live all by yourself . . . and whatever you may see or hear in the night you must not scream out, for if you give as much as a single cry my suffering will be doubled." To this the Princess agrees. After two years of horrifying experiences, through all of which she remains silent, the crow comes to her and adds,

"Before I can resume my natural form . . . you must go out into the world and take service as a maidservant."

This accomplished, the Prince is transformed and they too live happily ever after.

There are countless other variations on this theme, the most familiar found in the tale of *Beauty and the Beast*. In every instance we come upon the following conditions:

1. She must leave her people.
2. She must be totally dependent upon herself during her time of trial.
3. She must suffer silently.
4. She must live with a possessed creature.

In every instance the woman must marry the male principle in its most unseemly form in order to aid it in its transformation. It is interesting to note that the male principle is invariably cast in the form of a beast or monster. The problem, these tales appear to be telling us, is that the feminine in freeing herself must accept the raw instinctual portion of herself.

As with the myths discussed earlier, these fairy tales on the one hand reveal the nature of the split between the masculine and feminine principles and the necessity of redeeming the lost value of the Other. Because the male in our society has been allowed publicly to live out his instinctual side without fear of ostracization, during which time he must repress only the feeling-side of his psyche — the stratum of tears, warmth, affection and aestheticism which have come to be identified as feminine — because he has been allowed expression of his instinctual realm, his problem in transformation has to do with the "killing" and therefore transforming of the beast in order to redeem the feminine.

The woman on the other hand is taught at an early age to suppress if not repress the instinctual side of her nature, the "beastial" portion of her psyche, the expression of which *would* lead to public ostracization. The tales reveal that her problem calls for an acceptance of the beast within.

Again, in the realm of fairytales this time, we are warned that we have repressed the other half of our being. True, the feminine in these tales does not take on the negative connotations that we found in our religious texts as an inherent condition. But the idea that the feminine must *purposively* take on the qualities and conditions which bespeak degradation appears to indicate the presence of a compensatory law of the psyche which has become perverted into a "true and natural" depiction of the feminine and therefore of woman in general. That is, whereas the fairytale presents us with temporary and purposively adapted modes of activity the fabricators of myths, mystical systems, and *mores* have mistakenly portrayed these modes as *natural and inborn distinctions,* inescapable and permanent features of what we are to understand as the definitive statement regarding the makeup of the masculine and the feminine.

In other words, we have taken the portrayals of the masculine and the feminine at the highpoint of a transformative act and frozen them in mid-air, leaving ourselves with the one-sided ideas of the masculine as aggressive and out-going, dressed in battle-garb, and the feminine as docile and introverted, dressed in the fabric of scullery maid and housekeeper.

The tale of the Prince tells us of the nature of polarities inherent in the feminine, whereas the tale of the Princess tells us of the soul's experience of itself. The mythological themes of the soul's exile are here repeated at the level of secular story-telling. But it is the same story. The injured beast is myself in need of soul's caring, and that caring places the soul in a different position. It is through my difficulties that I become reconciled with what is defined as basic in the feminine. What I see through sees through me, too. The Prince and the Princess are a new Adam and Eve, both caught in the myth of myself where the two tales occur at one and the same time.

* * *

> Then she began to bark also, crawling after him — barking in a fit of laughter, obscene and touching. The dog began to cry then, running with her, head-on with her head, as if to circumvent her; soft and slow his feet went padding. He ran this way and that, low down in his throat crying, and she grinning and crying with him; crying in shorter and shorter spaces, moving head to head until she gave up, lying out, her hands beside her, her face turned and weeping; and the dog too gave up then, and lay down, his eyes bloodshot, his head flat along her knees.
> —from *Nightwood* by Djuna Barnes

* * *

We in the West have for too long been without passion. Modern man has dedicated himself to the furtherance of civilization — the construction of functional but fragile forms of reality. This impulse has been a significant factor in the extension of consciousness. It has aided us in the difficult task of establishing the perimeter of the rational and scientifically determinable portion of the phenomenal world. It has allowed us to escape from the collective night fears of history's childhood. But all of this and more has been accomplished at an enormous expense by virtue of the fact that it demanded the masculine and "rational" portion of our humanity come to the fore for the task. That is, the immediate and so-called "irrational" response to Being, that which the ancients identified as the Feminine, had to be put aside for us to accomplish what we have. But it is for this very reason that what has been accomplished is sometimes put to ends which lack the wisdom only emotion and passion can give us. In putting aside all that is not "rational," all that does not coincide with the light streaming from the sun of our egos, and in identifying the feminine with the term "irrational," we have buried a portion of ourselves in the gross earth of *avidya*, ignorance. And to make matters worse we have then taken this rash new formulation of the Feminine and identified it with women in general.

The alchemist understood not only the importance of the Feminine within, but also the necessity of attaining a viable relationship with the feminine without, a *soror mystica*, a wife as companion and worker. It was a very simple and unconscious premise, as most truths are: there are two sexes with two fundamentally unique functions. If the world is truly descended from and modelled after a trans-personal sphere, an archetypal dimension devoid of form as we know it, there we may expect to find two pulses of *equal* value — a plus and a minus, a yin and a yang, a systole and a diastole, a contraction and expansion which on this plane has been transcribed into a male and a female.

And here it is important to take note of these differences between the terms masculine/feminine and male/female. The former refer to psychic and spiritual modalities that should never have been *identified* with the latter biological terms.

It is only at this date, in the twentieth century, that the discoveries of the alchemists might be taken and applied. My point is that it is now possible, for the first time, to construct an alchemical yoga of sorts. But the initial risk in outlining such a discipline is in confining its creative and on-going process to fixed rules — and, even more dangerously, to socially determined images of Being. The very nature of alchemy demands that its expression be allowed to modify or amplify different aspects of the work in accordance with the needs or potentials of the worker. This cannot be done if the worker perceives himself or herself as a one-sided figure, fearful of accepting innate qualities because they have been deemed oppositional in nature to the socially prescribed role of the individual.

Ultimately, the alchemical process is Soul work and its aim is the opening of communications between solar and lunar consciousness.

> Know that our work requires a true change of natures, which cannot be unless the union of both these natures becomes absolute. Yet no such union may be, except after the manner of waters . . . this union is not of bodies . . . these do but grind together. . . . Yet of spirits between themselves such union well

may be; but to this end the homogeneous metallic water is required.
—from the *Hermetic Museum*

NOTES

[1]Kerenyi, Karl, *The Religion of the Greeks and Romans*, Greenwood Press Publishers, Westport, Connecticut, 1977, p. 115.

[2]Hillman, James, *Re-Visioning Psychology*, Harper & Row, New York, 1975, p. 140.

ON THE ANDROGYNE

I

Working with symbols is a dangerous business. More often than not our enthusiasm tends to conceal more than it reveals. The imagination that gripped us becomes gripped and slips out of our sight as quicksilver from a clenched fist. The greater the symbol, the greater the danger that this might happen with every interpretive thrust of our inquiry. The pages I am about to create are thick with such dangers, for in the figure of the androgyne we have a symbol almost too large for the meager art of interpretation. I must at the outset admit that what follows is the product of a thing imagined.

The focus of my imagination is the idea that there might be a formula for psychological or spiritual transformation. Its lineaments appear to be given us in religion, myths, spiritual traditions, our dream-life and history as process. The formula is a simple one: at the beginning of every psychological or spiritual process we are presented with a figure composed of the opposites in a state of union; at the middle of the process the opposites exist in a state of division, and at the end of the process the opposites are again united. In religion, mythology, and spiritual disciplines the beginning and end of this process are symbolized by a bi-sexual being.[1] However, because the figure appearing at the beginning is markedly different from that appearing at the end it is imperative that they be labeled and defined. The terms I will employ are familiar: hermaphrodite and androgyne.

There are a number of creation myths in which the establishment and demarcation of the world as we know it comes about through the forceful separation of two World Parents joined in what appears to be an endless state of sexual union. Invariably, we find their offspring angrily suffering the darkness and stasis of their newborn condition. In time, one of the children revolts and gets about the business of separating the pair forever, thereby bringing about all of those circumstances we tend to interpret as symbolic of consciousness: the sun appears, geographic points are established, heaven and earth become fixed locales, speech is invented, and human beings roam the earth. The emphasis these myths place on the tenacity of this couple's embrace and the effort needed finally to separate them, brings to my mind the image of a single bisexual figure, the hermaphrodite.

The special feature of this hermaphroditic creature is the fact that as long as it existed in an undivided state, the world and consciousness could not come into existence. It therefore represents a time that exists prior to the differentiation of psyche and soma. In short, such creation myths may be thought of as illustrating the psychological and biologic nature of the new-born infant. On the one hand, consciousness and the unconscious have not yet been established as two distinct fields, and on the other the recessive qualities of the organism have not yet been separated from the distinguishing biological characteristics of the human body. It was upon this latter reality that Jung based his theory of the anima and the animus:

> It is a well-known fact that sex is determined by a majority of male or female genes, as the case may be. But the minority of genes does not simply disappear. A man therefore has in him a

feminine side, an unconscious feminine figure. . . I have called this figure the "anima," and its counterpart in a woman the "animus."[2]

We may assume from this that the symbolism of the hermaphrodite in world literature not only refers us to the original unity of the anima/animus archetypes, but of the masculine and feminine in ourselves prior to their differentiation. Emphasis is placed on the genitals in both the archetypal instance, when we read of the creation myths dealing with the sexual union of the primal parents, and the biological instance, in which sexual differentiation is established.

The second stage is one in which the original double-sexed figure is divided. The splitting of the original unity, the T'ai Chi in Chinese philosophy, also gives birth to the opposites which in turn make manifest the universe. The sixth day of Genesis brings about the division of the hermaphroditic Adam into the opposites that will parent humankind. In every instance the splitting of the hermaphrodite leads to the birth of consciousness and of the world as we know it.[3] Thus, the price of consciousness is the original unity of the anima and the animus. The tension that we as humans experience between ourselves and between each other in regard to the idea of the masculine and the feminine is the wound that we would heal by realizing their unity.

The third stage in the pattern is symbolized by the opposites reunited, the major difference being that their union is depicted as asexual. In religious traditions this figure is always thought of as an intensification and broadening of our humanity, a time of unequivocal freedom symbolized as the result of a marriage sharply contrasting the sexual union of the hermaphrodite. This is the androgyne, in Western culture symbolized by the Christ.

We may therefore say that the hermaphroditic state is a given whereas the androgynous state is a realization. The hermaphrodite symbolizes the realm of the physical body, the somatic realm that borders the psyche, whereas the androgyne refers us to the subtle body and the archetypal realm. The term "hermaphrodite" describes an undesirable state of union, in that it is unconscious and static, in need of differentiation; while the term "androgyne" corresponds to our myth of a differentiated consciousness comprised of a union of opposites. And yet Jung warns us that the re-union of the masculine with the feminine may lead to an extinction of consciousness.[4] Here we reach a difficult juncture for it is often assumed that what is called for is the marriage of our manifest biological nature, with our recessive and psychological nature, which is to say the marriage of the male ego with the anima or the female ego with the animus. Obviously something different must occur. The myth that all we need do is marry ourselves to what is recessive in us falls apart when we read Jung's comment that the sacred marriage, and therefore the androgynous process,[5] does not take place "within the sphere of discriminating consciousness."[6]

> The anima and animus live in a world quite different from the world outside—in a world where the pulse of time beats infinitely slowly, where the birth and death of individuals count for little.[7]

The desire in anima and animus to take part in the world of consciousness that has been created through their separation, places upon us the responsibility of providing a proper stage for their manifestation. We might imagine that the interplay of these two archetypal figures gives shape to the soul in much the same manner that the interplay of the male and female in the world gives shape to our existence in the body. The more attention that we give to the construction of a proper stage setting, the greater the effect that the archetypes have on us, for ultimately it is their interaction that creates the drama and the comedy of our lives. Jung's statement that the union of these divine opposites occurs outside of consciousness implies that it is not my 'I-ness' as a male that must marry the archetype, but rather the conjunction of the animus with the anima. But if men have access only to the anima, and women only to the animus, how then are we to effect such a union—wherever such a union may occur? James Hillman noted this discrepancy in two papers on the anima which I feel clear up some major difficulties.

Simply put, Hillman states that the restricting of the anima to men and the animus to women is not tenable in the light of pure observation. The characteristics of the anima thought to be available only to men appear in women as well.[8] In addition, he points out that by restricting the concept of anima or of soul to men alone is to do nothing more than to maintain the traditional view that women are without soul, every image that would be defined as anima in a man's experience ending up as shadow in a woman's.[9]

The upshot of his observation is that the animus and the anima, or at least their effects, are equally available to both men and women. This somewhat helps us out of our difficulty—a conjunction of the anima/animus now theoretically possible within the area of one soul. It is no longer just a matter of the man's anima hooking up with a woman's animus. It can be that too, but it is clearly not *just* that.

It also helps to clear up another difficulty I believe must have plagued any number of people involved with Jungian ideas. Here I refer to the fact that while Jung often employed the symbolism of Chinese philosophy and Kundalini yoga to transpose his observations into psychological theory, the fact that these systems speak of the masculine (yang/Shiva) and feminine (yin/Shakti) as contained in both sexes did nothing to alter profoundly the one-archetype-to-one-sex theory. Hillman's reading of Jung and his redefining of the anima/animus theory finds support in the texts of ancient philosophy. The stumbling block to our perception of the sacred marriage and the androgyne comes simply from the problem of our transposing it into terms of ego and archetype, physical and transpersonal, I and that which is without 'I-ness.' All of which leads us to the next question: If the androgyne is not a happening in the field of ego-consciousness, where is it happening?

Jung tells us that the sacred marriage takes place in the alchemical substance Mercurius[10] and he adds that Mercurius is the hermaphroditic or bisexual figure that stands at both the beginning and the end of the alchemical process, that it is at once the prima materia and the philosopher's stone.[11] In other words, according to our definition, Mercurius is the hermaphrodite *and* the androgyne. In addition, he identifies Mercurius as the collective unconscious, the place of archetypal reality that at every moment impinges upon our world as we live it. Thus, the transformation of our hermaphroditic natures, as well as the healing of the split caused by the advent of consciousness, takes place *in* the androgyne. The androgyne is pre-existent. It is not something we create any more than we create the Mother or the Hero archetype. It is. If anything it creates us and we in our divided state can only hope to enter into participation with it through some type of method as yet not collectively perceived. The androgyne is a truly transpersonal reality, a subtle body whose existence must be awakened to.

To discover the geography of the androgyne we must first consider that Jung came to doubt the "exclusively psychic nature of the archetypes," finding them to have a nature that "cannot with certainty be designated as psychic."[12]

> ... the archetypes are not found exclusively in the psychic sphere, but can occur just as much in circumstances that are not psychic (equivalence of an outward physical process with a psychic one).[13]

If the archetypal world is not confined to the human soul but extends throughout the continuum of being and non-being, then we are faced with the fact that the experience of the androgyne as a subjective happening—the identification of myself as a happy union of masculine and feminine qualities—is illusory if it is not accompanied by a simultaneous occurrence of archetypally-toned phenomena in the world about me. That the similarity of such phenomena is a necessary adjunct to the activation of an archetype is the basis of Jung's definition of synchronicity.[14] The uniqueness of Jung's perception concerning the nature of synchronicity has in a way served to blind us to the simple reality of his theory. If I am present to a moment of synchronicity, a meaningful coincidence in which inner and outer worlds correspond, I am then contained in something different from the everyday world of consciousness. Henry Corbin puts us on to the situation in greater detail:

> Spiritual [i.e. archetypal or imaginal] bodies or entities are not *in* any world, nor *in* their world, in the same manner as a material body is in its place or may be contained in another body. On the contrary, their world is *in* them... Of course, all these entities subsist independently of each other. Nonetheless, all exist simultaneously and each is contained in the other.[15]

In other words, the activation of the androgyne is a moment in which we become contained in an androgynous world. What happens is that we then become capable of perceiving the androgyne, and it is the perception of this world that allows us the effect of the androgyne which in turns opens us to the possibility of such a consciousness.[16] I emphasize that it is solely a possibility, for the entry into the mercurial waters of the archetype becomes a revelatory happening in consciousness only if one can allow that everyday realities are penetrated through and through by archetypes— that, in the words of Evangelos Christou, "The psyche is not inside man, it is we who are inside the psyche."[17] James Joyce attempted

On the Androgyne

to alert us to this reality by having his hero, Leopold Bloom, live out the entire cycle of Ulysses' travels during the passage of one day. The comedy and tragedy of Bloom is that he never fully realizes that he moves in the midst of an archetypal world, that he himself has become the myth. So too do many of us float in our myths, the symbol of the androgyne being but one of many archetypes in a series of archetypal awakenings. William James suggested that human consciousness is one of many worlds.[18] These other worlds of consciousness are the archetypes.

> . . . the unseen region in question is not merely ideal, for it produces effects in this world. When we commune with it, work is actually done upon our finite personality, for we are turned into new men. . . But that which produces effects within another reality must be termed a reality itself . . .[19]

So what we are discussing is the problem of perceiving ourselves *in* the androgyne. We must somehow become capable of seeing through the opaqueness of ego-consciousness and into the realm of archetypal happenings, or perceiving that the symbol, the image, is a world of consciousness in its own right and not something that we create out of hand. I do not mean to imply by the foregoing, however, that this suggested imaginal three-fold processes of transformation solely occurs in the archetypal realm. I am on the side of the Chinese who say that the process of becoming manifests itself through the world of humanity (inter-personal relationships), earth (the demands of being-in-the-world), and heaven (the archetypal or imaginal realm).[20]

At the interpersonal level, for example, when two people come together in love in a way that causes an inexpressible feeling of romantic oneness to encompass and contain them both, we can assume that they have entered the hermaphroditic world. Their immersion in each other to the exclusion of their individual differences (which as we all know are put aside at such moments), blurs the person. The urge of the anima and animus to unite in one body draws us out of ourselves and into a conjunction through which our souls attempt to find their other halves outside of us in projected form. In time the projection begins to fade and we slowly and painfully notice the all too human differences that exist between ourselves and those who have received our projection. Such projections, in turn, tend to become prisons for the recipient. Suddenly demands are made to fulfill the soul-image projected upon us and we rebel, separate; we suddenly find ourselves in the midst of divisive issues where once there had been total agreement and unity. The second phase of the process has begun and its successful completion is dependent upon the integrity, consciousness, and emotional capacity of each party finally to perceive one another outside of the hermaphroditic world. That such separations inevitably occur suggests that the androgyne cannot be realized until the withdrawal of our soul-projections are realized. When I know where I begin and end and where the other person begins and ends, then I and the other are on the way to the world of the androgyne.

In the meantime the withdrawal of my projection leads me towards conflicting doubts about the nature and reality of my soul in general — "How could I have fallen in love with such a person?" we ask. This expulsion from the Paradise of the hermaphrodite signals the first step towards a consciousness of our situation. If one can sustain the tension of growing out of this separation the inward pull of the withdrawn projection eventually leads us towards the other half of the soul within us for entry into the androgynous world. What this means in the area of relationships is that whereas in the hermaphroditic phase of our coming together there was one, in the androgynous phase there are three — two individuals and the third thing that unites them in consciousness.[21]

By the same token, at the level of our relationships with the business of being-in-the-world, I can become hermaphroditic, individual, and androgynous in regard to my job, my ideas, even my pastimes. We are all familiar with the businessman or the housewife who become identified with their jobs to the exclusion of themselves as individuals.

It goes without saying that political, sociological, and psychological approaches to the world of the androgyne will effect change in our social philosophies. In the long run such platforms will have little effect on our souls if the archetype itself is not dealt with in what Corbin has defined as the realm of the imaginal, where the image resides. For this, he adds, one must call upon the aid of an "organ of trans-sensory imagination."[22] In that Jung said that the basis of all consciousness is the image,[23] entry into the world of the androgyne demands that each of us perform an active imagination over the nature of our interiority as well as the archetypal ground that everywhere surrounds us. It is there, in the imaginal, where the androgyne resides, and it is there where we must journey if we are to bring ourselves to a consciousness that may truly be called androgynous.

But we have several problems to overcome, for ever since the close of the seventeenth century, and certainly ever since the advent of modern psychology, we have had a deep-seated fear of confusing the imaginal with the ego-world—and not without good reason I must add. What has happened, however, is that we presently have psychologies that seek to cut us off from the imaginal, to make us wholly conscious, invulnerable to imagination and the archetypes.

But invulnerability means that one cannot be touched, and if one cannot be touched one cannot be psychologically moved. The fear of the imaginal becomes a pathology in itself, a withdrawal of the ego from all that is dark, unknown, and sensual in favor of that which is light, distant and above-it-all, in control. Ego-consciousness is won at the price of depth of soul. What is peculiar to humanity—its awareness of suffering, its pathos and its comedy, its ability to endure the sometimes painful reality of Being—becomes coated over by a myth of happiness-is-healthiness. The intrusion of images and phantasies onto the screen of consciousness becomes something we should rid ourselves of, in true yogic fashion. Consciousness becomes equated with not only happiness but psychic blankness. My nightmares should be ignored and my anxieties tranquilized. The mental clinic becomes a place where people are corrected rather than connected or understood. I am told that if I want to get in touch with my anger (and therefore with something that is primal and connects me with the base of psyche) I should use a punching bag, or become verbally abusive to my wife, my employer, my children. Action replaces perception.

But none of the prescriptions given us today by either psychology, religion, philosophy or even a good friend puts us in contact with the androgyne. The only thing that puts us in contact with that archetype is the very thing everyone tries to cure us of— the conflict of the opposites in their divisive state. What we have not yet fully developed is a method by which we may finally marry the opposites again, safely.

I have reached the end of my first imagining, the major attempt of which was to suggest a definition of the terms hermaphrodite and androgyne, propose that there exists a threefold process of psychological transformation, repeat the oft-stated policy that there are indeed other worlds of consciousness, and imply that where there is another world of consciousness, there must also be another method for the attainment of that consciousness.

II

Tantric tradition tells us that prior to the creation of all things the Great Lord Shiva existed in his unmanifest form of Parashiva, void of all distinctions. Contained within this sexless first principle were an inactive principle that would in time come to be regarded as the father of the universe, and an active principle that would become known as the mother.[24] But this ever-changeless Being had a *Kama* (desire) to be an ever-changing seeming and thereby took on the role of relative becoming. As one text tells us, this *Kama* gave rise to the active feminine principle, the Primordial Shakti, who in adoration of Her Lord turned herself into a "Pure mirror in which Shiva experiences Himself."[25] Upon this mirror fell the rays of Parashiva as the sun. The substance of these rays, inactive in itself, was then carried by the energic-reflection of the Shakti, each reflection causing a diminution of the Divine feminine, to create a series of worlds, or tattvas of which there are thirty-six. This series of manifestations are understood as the *"stages of evolution of the One into the Many as Mind and matter"*.[26] With the manifestation of the 36th tattva, the earth, Shakti's creativity came to a close as she, in the form of a serpent, entered the grossness of matter to sleep. In this form the feminine is known as Kundalini-Sakti, and the Earth that she slumbers in is the human body.[27] In such a manner does the microcosm come into being. The macrocosm (*Mahabramanda*), composed of the sacred mountain Meru and fourteen worlds — of which seven are imagined as upper, and seven as nether or lower — is the model for the human body. Mt. Meru is the spinal column and the seven upper worlds become seven centers or chakras located along its length. The seven nether worlds are imagined as existing below the first chakra (the *muladhara*) "and in the joints, sides, anus, and organs of generation".[28] The personal soul (*purusha*) we are told corresponds with the cosmic soul (*Hiranyagarbha*).

It is believed the life force of the individual is dispersed through the two channels of *Ida* and *Pingala*, the moon and the sun channels respectively.[29] We may think of these channels as symbolic of Eros and Logos. The sun channel may be imagined as symbolizing either an extraverted and dispassionate manner of dealing with the world or as the source of volatile impulses. By the same token, the moon channel may be imagined as symbolizing either an introverted and impassioned manner of dealing with the world or as the source of corrosive compulsions. The object of Kundalini yoga is to liberate oneself from the unconscious activities of the sun and the moon channels by withdrawing the energy contained within them. The retrieved energies are then shuttled up the central channel with the aid of Kundalini.[30] The withdrawal of these energies activates the sleeping serpent causing it to rise up through the central channel, activating and purifying the chakras until it enters into a sacred union with the masculine principle.[31]

Anyone who has ever entered into a yogic regimen will readily admit that what has been described above is no mere illusion. The psychological effects of this discipline are pronounced as are the many psychic disturbances that sometimes arise. But the most curious thing about this yoga is not that there are effects, but that the entire process begins *through an assiduous application of imagination*. Practically the whole of the Yoga Upanishads[32] concerns itself with the description of what is to be internally *seen* by the yogin in his practice. It is not without interest to note that the creation of the world in Tantricism is spoken of as a product of creative imagination. We are told that Shiva and Shakti represent the static and kinetic aspects of consciousness and that the power that brings the dualistic world into being, Maya-Sakti, is actually a veiling and projecting principle.[33] It is for this reason that the world is called an imagination (*Kalpana*) and Shakti is imagined as a consciousness that imagines (*Srsti-kalpana*) the world into being. The dualistic world comes into being through a process of Creative Imagination. Thus entry into the world of the subtle body and the Androgyne is accomplished through the feminine, the Shakti/Anima. It is important to remember that Tantric myth tells us the world came into existence through the agency of the anima as mirror, as reflector. We must also call to mind Jung's statement that the instincts fall into five major groups: hunger, sexuality, activity, creativity, and reflection.[34] About this latter instinct he wrote, "Reflection is the cultural instinct *par excellence*, and its strength is shown in the power of culture to maintain itself in the face of untamed nature."[35] Jung's reasons for identifying reflection as an instinct are as follows: the instinct of activity, or rather its drive, is in humans transfered by a moment of deliberation or reflection before its carry-over into action. At least, this is the idealized state of humanity. We train our dogs into mimicking something like a state of reflection that cause them to go against their instinctual impulse to attack with commands such as "sit" or "halt." But true reflection is a specifically human instinct and one that the Tantric texts inform us is an innate activity of the anima. Jung said much the same:[36]

> Where judgements and flashes of insight are transmitted by unconscious activity, they are often attributed to an archetypal feminine figure, the anima or mother-beloved.[37]

Also: "The richness of the human psyche and its essential character are probably determined by this reflective instinct."[38] To which Hillman adds, "This psyche is mainly a result of the instinct of reflection, which in turn is intimately tied with the anima archetype," and quoting from Jung again:

> ... reflection is a spiritual act that runs counter to the natural process; an act whereby we stop, call something to mind, form a picture, and take up a relation to and come to terms with what we have seen. It should, therefore, be understood as an act of becoming conscious.[39]

Wrapping it up for our purposes here, one final quote from Hillman:

> If 'becoming conscious' has its roots in reflection and if this instinct refers to the anima archetype, then consciousness itself may more appropriately be conceived as based upon anima than upon ego.[40]

What is truly curious is that all of these very learned psychological statements and observations are contained in our Tantric myth. The human world, and thus human consciousness, comes into being through a reflective act on the part of the Shakti/Anima. In addition, each chakra is thought of as governing one of the senses[41] and therefore symbolic of *a* consciousness, so the call for the repeated passage of the Kundalini/anima through these centers suggests that the anima is behind our sensory appreciation of the world—behind our very "earthiness." But the implications do not end here if we recall that the Tantric text calls for an image of the Parasiva figure to become located in the head of humans, its model being the Macrocosmic Parasiva. This microcosmic Parasiva becomes the ego of Western psychology which Jung tells us is but a small model of the Self.[42]

The Shiva/ego is therefore an unreflective aspect of consciousness that is incapable of perceiving itself without the intervention of the Shakti/anima's appearance as reflector. Without reflection and imagination the ego's perception of the world is without substance, airy. Jung put it nicely when he wrote that "Matter represents the concreteness of God's thoughts,"[43] for religious tradition tells us that the feminine *is* matter. Without reflection there is no substance, without anima there is only a blank seeing. Therefore ego-consciousness alone cannot lead us to the realization of the androgyne. Because the androgyne is composed of both the masculine and feminine, it demands a masculine and a feminine consciousness to perceive it. Reflection and imagination are the trans-sensory organs of the perception that Corbin observed is needed for a greater consciousness.

We must now consider the statements given us concerning the manifestation of the Shakti through the worlds. Hindu commentators call this activity of the Shakti/anima a dimming of Shiva consciousness in that the rays of Shiva's body become clothed with the Mayanic energy of the feminine. Consciousness is equated with the masculine and unconsciousness with the feminine—a thesis in no way peculiar to modern Western psychology also, as unsettling as it must be to women. The final act in the creation myth leaves us with the image of the depleted feminine tucked away at the base of the human body. I suggest that the glorious descriptions of Kundalini's beauty given us by the Hindu not detract us from the fact that the feminine has essentially become at this point a sleeping beauty of the alimentary zones. A number of religious traditions in the West also tell us of a spiritual masculine principle residing on high, in a fixed position of centrality, from which the feminine has become separated. The Gnosticism of Justin informs us that the creator of the universe, Elohim, deserted his wife Eden so that he could ascend towards a light brighter than the sun. The desertion brings about a desire for revenge on his wife's part that leads to the human ills of adultery, general sin, and evil to flourish on the earth with which she is (as the Kundalini) identified.[44]

Yet another doctrine, that of Simon, has it that the First Thought, that which leaped towards the nether regions to create the world after the plan of her Father's will, was held captive on earth by the angels and powers she created. She in time suffers the final humiliation by becoming trapped in a human body to undergo numerous incarnations, "Always suffering disgrace from it . . . until she was manifest in a prostitute."[45] The myth of Jewish mysticism, Kabbalism, has it that the feminine portion of God, the Shekhinah, is trapped in the lower of four worlds (*asiyah*) where only evil spirits and mankind dwell. As in the Gnostic and Tantric myth, she too is symbolized by and identified with the earth.

The major feature of all these myths (and others too numerous to recount here) is that the dimming of the bright light of consciousness (as in the Tantric myth) is brought about by the creation of the human world, and is in one way or another the cause of the feminine. The suggestion in all of these myths is that the Divine business cannot be completed until the feminine returns to the sphere of the masculine, and return under her own power, no less. If we consider these myths in our imaginal formula for transformation, the separation out of the hermaphroditic state that brings about consciousness, the opposites, and individuality occurs because of the feminine. *But this occurrence is seen as a fault.* The masculine rejects the whole affair out of hand and goes about its immovable centeredness. It is as if every gain in ego-consciousness must be countered by a pulling away from and rejection of the imaginative and reflective qualities of the anima. The masculine is content merely to perceive the suffering that these many myths inform us the anima undergoes in her exile. Jung, commenting upon a similar depiction of the Sophia in yet another Gnostic tale, notes that such a condition clearly characterizes "the anima of a man who identifies himself absolutely with his reason and his spirituality."[46] The inevitable result of this is a dissociation from the anima and the compensatory healing powers of the unconscious in general, thereby cutting himself off from, "on the one hand the anima as the connecting link with the world beyond and the eternal images, while on the other hand her emotionality which involves man in the chthonic world and its transitoriness."[47]

The fixity of the masculine in all of these myths, the demand that the feminine get herself out of her predicament, means that the masculine "is content to merely perceive psychic suffering, but does not make itself conscious of the reasons behind it."[48]

What we are faced with is a predicament in which the birth of consciousness also causes a displacement and depreciation of the very thing that gave rise to it. These ancient myths reveal the attitude towards the unconscious that consciousness would eventually take. In turn, the rejection of the anima in our psyches becomes the rejection of the female in the world. We should also consider that these myths anticipated if not predicted the predicament of twentieth-century consciousness. If this is indeed the case, then we must be able to discover somewhere in these imaginal systems the next development in consciousness, or at the very least the nature of our present condition at the collective level.

The estrangement of the anima from the animus is depicted in the Kundalini system by the figure of the slumbering Kundalini in the *muladhara* chakra. In the Kabbalistic system of the Sefiroth, we also discover that the Shekhinah is essentially unconscious in that she lives in a world of evil darkness. In both instances the home of the feminine is the element earth. The upward movement these feminine principles must undertake represents the third phase in our imaginal process of transformation only in that it is a step towards union. Archetypally speaking, this is a movement towards the world of the androgyne. But before we can begin an attempt to see if we may indeed discover where we are in terms of these two imaginal systems it would do us well to consider some observations that Jung made concerning the Chakra system.[49]

Jung first turns our attention to the second chakra to suggest that its symbolism of ocean and sea-monster answers our twentieth-century Western description of the unconscious. He goes on to say that this second chakra might therefore be called "the chakra or mandala of baptism, or of rebirth, or of destruction, whatever the consequence of baptism might be."[50] In other words, it symbolizes everything that happens to us when we meet the unconscious. Then he turns his attention to the first chakra, (*muladhara*), and asks us to reconsider its symbolism.

Identifying the second chakra as the unconscious is a fairly simple matter, for it contains all of the elements symbolic of the night-sea journey, but the first chakra presents some problems in that a Westerner would immediately assume it too symbolizes the unconscious. Its element is earth, its name is the "root support," it contains a phallus and slumbering serpent, and it is a symbol of what *is* unconscious. But what *is* unconscious isn't necessarily *the* unconscious. The symbolism tells us that with this chakra "we are in the region of the roots of our existence on this earth."[51] In other words, muladhara is the earth mandala and represents "where mankind is a victim of impulses, instincts, unconsciousness . . . *participation mystique*."[52] What is unconscious in this mandala is not *the* unconscious but the Self.

This leads to the possibility that muladhara is located in our heads and not in the perianal region: that the entire chakra system becomes inverted in the West.[53] Thus the idea that the second chakra is below us rather than above us (as in the Eastern system) corresponds with the psychological facts of the Western world: the way to the unconscious is down not up, in not out.[54] Jung's re-alignment of the Chakra system fits in with everything that we have said about the condition of the feminine at the apogee of her separation from the masculine. The world she slumbers in is indeed the unconscious of the Gods and it is not until the feminine is awakened that the possibility of their recognition as vital factors in humanity might again come to pass. It is through the faculty of a re-awakened active and creative imagination that we might again come into contact with the imaginal.

In the light of Jung's statement identifying the first chakra—and therefore the first sefirah of the Kabbalistic system as well—with the unconscious, let us now consider the next point of reference. That the first chakra and the first sefirah coincide is an interesting coincidence at first sight. A close look at the coincidence of the Svadhisthana chakra and the Yesod sefirah leads us into deeper waters. Both are symbolized by the genitals and both represent the first attempt at a reconciliation of the opposites. If the muladhara chakra is indeed located in the head, in the field of our everyday Western consciousness, and if the myth of estrangement from the anima is aptly depicted in our masculine attitude towards the unconscious and the anima, then what does it mean that the unconscious in both of these systems is identified by the genitals? What is there about the twentieth-century psyche that in any way corresponds with this symbolism?

Consider this: if there is any one idea that has changed the whole of twentieth-century thought right down to the awareness

On the Androgyne

of the high school freshman, if there is any one myth that has gripped the imagination of the entire civilized Western world, it is the myth of this ephemeral thing we call the unconscious. The myth of the unconscious represents the first awakening of the Kundalini/anima in that it called forth every ounce of Western imagination to accept it as a philosophical probability. With the advent of this theory the movement towards the androgyne began. It was only fitting that we should move towards the imaginal with an imaginal concept. Consider this further: *the* prominent myth of the unconscious today, that which every housewife and businessman, laborer, scholar, and philosopher could name without fail on any quiz show is the Freudian myth. It would therefore profit us to take a brief look at Freud within the context of everything we have said up to this point.

Freud came to the realization of one of his most important contributions through his dissatisfaction with the technique of hypnotic suggestion.[55] In his attempt to deal with the problem of post-hypnotic amnesia, he persuaded his patients to free-associate by closing their eyes and concentrating on memory recall. Conscious associations were to be put aside in favor of the spontaneous images that came to mind. In other words, he intuited that the way into the unconscious was through imagining—for every memory comes to us via the image. If any of us should attempt to remember what it was that we had for supper two evenings ago we would have to rely on an imagining of the meal—on a "seeing" of the past. The act of free-association thereby came to define the psychiatric process. The time spent with my analyst was a time spent imagining. The creation of the space called a psychoanalytic hour came into existence through the type of reflection we saw Shakti perform in creating the world. The world of my analysis is created through the activity of the anima imagining, through the feminine reflecting what will in time become the substance of not only my analysis but myself as well.

The next important observation that Freud made was that within every neurosis there were to be found delusional phantasies, i.e. imaginings, and that it is these phantasies themselves that give rise to symptoms of both a physiological and physical nature.[56] The source of all such phantasies we are told is the masturbatory phase of childhood.[57] And, finally, all symptoms have their origin in "the expression of both a masculine and a feminine unconscious sexual phantasy," or what he referred to as a bisexual nature.[58] In other words, the proddings of the phantasies behind a neurosis might be likened to the proddings of those children in our creation myths who attempt to bring about the separation of their hermaphroditic parents. The separation of my ego from the compulsive aspect of the unconscious leads to a consciousness of who and what I am. The bi-sexual activity Freud referred to may be likened to the hermaphroditic being composed of the anima and the animus prior to their separation. Every neurosis is a hermaphrodite attempting to become an androgyne.

The framework within which Freud worked appears to be even more archetypal than we tend to recognize when we consider his theory of libido. In *An Outline of Psychoanalysis*, he writes that there are two basic instincts, Eros and the destructive instinct, which he later called Thanatos.[59] He tells us that the aim of Eros—which he quickly renames libido[60]—"is to establish ever greater unities and to preserve them thus—in short, to bind together."[61]

The expression of this libido, furthermore, streams into the ego "from the various organs and parts of the body,"[62] the most prominent portions called the erotogenic zones. Strictly speaking, he adds, the entire body is an erotogenic zone.[63] The technique of psychoanalysis is one of freeing up libido which has flowed back to an early stage of human development. The regression of this "life force" was thought of by him as the cause of psychic illness.

Eros, or what Freud came to call libido, was according to two Greek accounts the first God to appear after the creation of the primal parents. He was to the Greek mind what he was in part to Freud, the cement of the world. In the same manner that he appears at the beginning of the world in Greek mythology, so too may he be thought of as being actively present in muladhara. He is both the blinding and binding force that keeps us rooted in the world. *Participation mystique* is a phenomenon of Eros. To fall in step with a collective mood is to fall in Love with that mood. Falling *in* love means just that—becoming encompassed by the archetype. This great, powerful, and all encompassing God of the Greeks in time became the infantile Cupid of Roman and modern times. The power of loving and its full expression became reduced to the capricious past-time, the masturbatory myth personified, of the infant. It is this end of the myth that Freud emphasized in his theory of the libido. In that theory, Eros is no longer a divine archetypal power that grips us, he is a compulsive seeking of pleasure that must undergo a process of maturation.

Here we have the myth complete. The maturation process is one in which libido becomes centered in and passes through three erotogenic zones: the mouth, the anus, and the penis, in that order. All three zones are described as "sexual" in that pleasure in one form or another is obtained from them during the development of the child.[64] The oral, anal, and phallic phases of maturation come to a close during early childhood to later give place to the genital phase of puberty. A further point of interest is that in the phallic phase "what comes in question . . . is not the genitals of both sexes but only those of the male. . . The female genitals long remain unknown."[65] This is a remarkable statement—the implication that the female child is more aware of the phallus than the reality of her own body. The fact that Freud who had much to say about our infantile origins never analyzed a child[66] can suggest only that such a treatment arose out of an imagining about the mythical or archetypal nature of things that he then literally applied to psychology in general.[67]

I strongly feel that the theory of libido and its development through the oral, anal, and phallic phases all have their origin in the archetypal configuration given us in the first chakra of Kundalini yoga. It is in that chakra where the totally unconscious nature of the Kundalini is symbolized by the image of her mouth encircling the susumna channel while her body itself lies entwined around a phallus. The location of this chakra—between the anus and the genitals—completes our Freudian picture. The final phase of maturation that Freud spoke of, the genital phase in which the sexual organs of both male and female are realized rather than the phallic alone, corresponds with the localization of the second chakra in the genital area. It is here too that the free-association method, the activation of unconscious contents, finds correspondence.

If nothing else Freud was called to the archetype to begin the modern myth-making process of transformation. His psychology of the genitals was a fulfillment of a development in the stages of consciousness intimated in the anthropomorphic figures of the Sefirothic and Kundalini Yoga systems. The revelation that the psyche gave us in the guise of a threefold system of transformation was as follows: first there will come to pass the myth of a world without archetypes that will then become a reality through the fashioning of a culture and a consciousness that thoroughly entertains this viewpoint, a mulhadharic consciousness. The historian of religions Mircea Eliade has commented upon this event in the following:

> It should be said at once that the completely profane world, the wholly desacralized cosmos, is a recent discovery in the history of the human spirit. . . Desacralization pervades the entire experience of the nonreligious man of modern societies and . . . in consequence, he finds it increasingly difficult to rediscover the existential dimensions of religious man in the archaic societies."[68]

This desacralization of the world, the death of God announced only a few short years ago in our weeklies, appears to be a necessary stage in the evolution of consciousness. Yet, our threefold model of transformation informs us that with the arrival of a consciousness that explains itself in terms of the symbolism of the genitals as well as the idea of the superiority of the masculine and the inferiority of the feminine, there will begin a movement towards the androgynic world.

We earlier discussed the idea that it is more a matter of entering the world of an archetype than it is of constellating an archetype within us. At that time I stressed that everything about oneself takes on the tone of the archetype in question. This is what has happened to us through the vehicle of Freudian theories. Our world is now encompassed by the Freudian myth of Oedipal conflicts, anality, penis envy, and the inferiority of both the feminine and the female. Much of the blame for our condition is heaped on the head of Freud rather than on our own heads for failing to perceive that what now grips us is the very thing that gripped him: an archetypal process of transformation whose value and meaning can be perceived only through a constant awareness of the androgyne as a symbol of a final becoming, as a symbol of a final development of consciousness. That history continually presents us with this androgynic figure as exemplary of a completion (right up to the present religious figure of the androgynous Christ) should have alerted us long ago.

I close my second imagining with the following observations: the mythic systems of the Sefiroth in Kabbalism and Kundalini Yoga in Tantricism display a process of becoming within the framework of an anthropomorphic figure. This figure is at once symbolic of an imaginal transpersonal body and our own bodies. Contained therein are stages that define the development of consciousness not only along subjective lines, but along historical and collective lines as well. In addition, we may assume that the appearance of this anthropomorphic figure in history may have coincided with the establishment of consciousness at the collective and evolutionary level. Thus the figure is a method that the psyche has given us for perceiving the manner by which the opposites that were divided at the birth of consciousness may again be united. Finally, the appearance of psychology as a science of psyche indicates that for the first time since the emergence of the phenomenon of human consciousness a movement towards the union of these opposites has begun. All that is needed is a re-evaluation of the feminine in ourselves and the female in the world. Without this, the experiment of psyche will fail.

III

Kundalini yoga was obviously one attempt on the part of the psyche to present us with an imaginal psychology—a method by which we could enter the world of the archetypes and participate in the spiritual and evolutionary character of the psyche firsthand. In contrast with many of our twentieth-century psychologies that deal with the Shiva aspect of consciousness—the extension of consciousness from a fixed center, the development of ego, the strengthening of personality—Kundalini yoga appears to concern itself with the dynamics of soul: with imagination, with psychic deepening, with unity, the body, and God. Jung was much attracted to this science of the soul and often made reference to it stating that there existed amazing parallels between it and his experience with the Western psyche. Yet, he warned us against actively applying a method with foreign roots on many occasions.[69] The fact that such similarities were found by Jung indicates that the West could easily develop an imaginal psychology similar in construction to Kundalini yoga. Jung wrote:

> In the course of the centuries the West will produce its own yoga, and it will be on the basis laid down by Christianity. It is more than likely that the yoga natural to the European proceeds from historical patterns unknown to the East.[70]

I now turn your attention back to Jung's comments concerning the nature of the chakra systems in the West. Muladhara, the chakra of the rejected and slumbering Kundalini/anima, is for us located in the field of our consciousness, in the domain of the ego-world. The suggestion is that our mundane view of psyche traps the anima in the field of ego. Her original reflective power has been diminished and parodied by the ego in the think-tank type of reflection we too often pass off as creative thinking. But true creative thinking the myths tell us cannot come to pass without the operations of the anima as reflector. Yet, the myth of modern consciousness tells us that the feminine is not only abased but without power. We therefore find the Freudian myth informing us that women are incapable of developing a strong superego — a theory created in an attempt to explain the then prevailing view that women naturally have a weak moral nature.[71] The original Jungian view that the anima is available only to men did little to help correct the matter, I must add.[72]

This image of the reflective feminine contained and imprisoned by the masculine, swallowed up and limited by ego, is given us in one of the myths of Zeus. We are told that Zeus was warned that the daughter of Okeanus, Metis, whom he had taken as a mistress, would one day give birth to a child or something stronger than his lightning. In the hope of circumventing his fate, Zeus swallowed Metis, trapping her in his stomach. What he didn't know was that she was pregnant and that the cause of his severe headaches shortly afterwards was the issue of their union seeking to be born. Aid was brought with the plunging of a double-ax into his head to release — armour shining like a thousand suns — the goddess Athena.

If one recalls Jung's statement to the effect that the ego is but a small model of the Self, also keeping in mind the Tantric belief that the Parasiva has its duplicate in the world, in our heads, then Zeus might be seen as a perfect model for the Western Ego. Argumenttative, ready to strike down all who go against his wishes, seducer, and supreme judge, Zeus in these aspects fits in many ways the description of what goes on in the Western offices of power. It is here that we find the daughter of Metis ("wise counsel"), of insight and reflection, banging at the door of ego-consciousness to get out.

Athena was known as the goddess who gave courage to the warrior, who replaced passion with reason and reflection thereby

On the Androgyne

causing many a hero to put up his sword rather than impulsively strike. Whereas her mother symbolized practical understanding, she represents illuminating clarity. She therefore brings another dimension of perception to the masculine through reflection. Myth tells us that it was only his gazing at the reflection of the Medusa in his shield that saved Perseus from becoming petrified. The shield is a symbol of Athena and the myth suggests that the petrifying quality that the unconscious sometimes holds for consciousness can be overcome only through the anima's gift of reflection. As Walter Otto has described Athena, she is "the heavenly presence and direction as illumination and inspiration to victorious comprehension and consummation."[73]

In Kundalini yoga the arrival of the Kundalini in the sixth chakra and her union with Shiva, the sacred marriage, releases a flood of ambrosia that anoints and illuminates the interior of the body, or psyche. I would like to suggest that the splitting open of the head of Zeus and the brilliance accompanying the emergence of Athena symbolize the same moment — the release of this feminine principle of reflection, and therefore the completion of an androgynic consciousness. But if in the Tantric system of Kundalini yoga it is the feminine that travels upward to meet the masculine, what then is it that travels upwards in our system to liberate the feminine?

We have already indicated that the ajna chakra, because of the inversion of the chakra system in our psyches, ends up where muladhara should be, in the genital zone. It was also implied that the Shiva principle who resides in that chakra becomes localized in that zone. If indeed our Kundalini/anima may be identified as Athena, who then might be identified with the Shiva? I return to the East for one final myth.

Vishnu, "the anthropomorphic embodiment of this fluid of life,"[74] is found floating in his own essence when he sees another luminous apparition approaching him at a great speed. There suddenly stands before him the "fashioner of the universe," Brahma, who immediately asks the reclining God who he is. Vishnu explains that he is the creator and destroyer of the universe. Brahma retorts that he is, and not Vishnu. As the two argue there suddenly appears out of the ocean an enormous lingam crowned with flame. It grows into infinity. Neither Brahma nor Vishnu can see the beginning or end of this phallus. They decide to investigate.

Vishnu plunges downward in the form of a boar and Brahma flies upward in the shape of a gander. They can find no end to the lingam. Suddenly it bursts open to reveal the great Lord Shiva who proclaims that he is the origin of them both, Super-shiva "the triad of Brahma, Vishnu, and Shiva."[75] Thus the phallus and Shiva symbolize the creative masculine principle of the universe—which "procreates and sustains the universe."[76] He is therefore not only the creator, but the active spiritual principle in nature. In Greek mythology three Gods are represented by the phallus, one of them symbolizing the active and dynamic principle in nature—the great god Pan who is in several ways connected with the other two phallic Gods Dionysus and Hermes.

The phallic nature of the god Hermes appears to have arisen from his depiction as god of the stone-heap, *herma*. Herms, later replaced with ithyphallic busts of the God, were employed as markers along paths and crossroads. Hermes himself was regarded as "the friendliest of gods to men,"[77] bestower of fruitfulness, shepherd of the flocks, and the guide to the underworld. Today he might be thought of as a guide to the unconscious. Myth tells us that he fell in love with a nymph who in time gave birth to their son Pan. Pan means "All," a name given him by the gods because the goat-footed and horned child pleased them all. He pleased the God Dionysus so much that the latter took the young Goat-god into his service. Pan we are told is the God of Nature who gives birth to panic, nightmares, is the inventor of masturbation, and a rapist. As James Hillman has defined the archetype,

> Pan's world is in a continual state of subliminal panic just as it is in a continual state of subliminal sexual excitation. As the world is made by Eros, held together by the cosmogonic force and charged with the libidinal desire that is Pan . . . so its other side, panic . . . belongs to the same constellation.[78]

As for Dionysus, Plutarch informs us that the Egyptians also represented Osiris as ithyphallic and that he was the same God as the Bacchus (Dionysus) of Greek mythology along with the God Eros of Orpheus.[79] The emblem of this God's celebration were "a wine jar, a vine, a goat, a basket of figs, and then the phallus."[80] We also know that a large phallus was displayed in the processions held in honor of the God at Delos and that every Greek colony regularly forwarded a phallus to the Athenian temple.

On the Androgyne

Hermes is the God of the underworld, he who leads us into the darkness of ourselves, pointing the path out; Pan is the God of Nature, of the primordial root of our instinctual lives; he rapes the naive psyche out of innocence, he is the masturbator; Dionysus, revealed to us in myth as a bisexual figure, is God of intoxication, liberator of our passions, the god of our darkness. All three of these Gods *are* the phallus. All three compose the figure of our Shiva in the West.

One other thing to consider is the fact that the serpent in the West is masculine. Alexander the Great was believed to have been the son of a serpent, as was Augustus.[81] The serpent of Eden was masculine, as are the snakes of the divine healer Asklepios. This latter figure was himself thought of as having sexual union with barren women in his snake form.[82] All of this is important in light of the fact that the constant companion of Athena was a snake,[83] and that the guardian demon of the Akropolis at Athens was the male serpent Erechtheus. An enormous statue of the Goddess with this serpent companion once stood on the Akropolis.[84] Therefore Athena and the masculine serpent are intimately connected in the same manner that Shiva is connected with Shakti in serpent form. The location of the ajna chakra in our Western version of the Kundalini system contains three phallic gods who represent the total function of Super-shiva. But what really ties this imagining up for me is the fact that one of these phallic gods was also given birth to by Zeus out of his own body—Dionysus. Whereas Athena was born from his head, Dionysus was born from his thigh: the masculine in the lower zone, the feminine in the higher, as Jung has suggested. By virtue of the fact that the two were born out of the body of their father, Dionysus and Athena may be thought of as brother and sister, as were Shiva and Shakti. And they represent a dichotomy: the sister symbolizes clarity and reflection, the brother ecstasy and freedom from reflection. Two sides of the same coin one might say.

Because I had been privileged to see a number of dreams by women in which the Kundalini presented itself as masculine, I was at first tempted to say that the masculine Kundalini was a phenomenon of feminine psychology alone. In the light of the above, however, I now strongly feel that the masculinity of the Kundalini applies to male psychology as well. The symbolism of the ensnared feminine is a collective problem shared by both men and women alike. All of this leads us to consider that we are today faced not only with the freeing of the feminine, but the resurrection of another kind of masculinity. Where anima is, animus is; any change in the nature of the one brings about a complementary change in the other. The portrayal of the masculine as that which is pure, solar, up there, unemotional, dry, and rational, always on target does not completely fit what we know about men. Obviously, during the creation of our Western model of masculinity a lot was left out. What was left out was the dark, emotional, instinctual, street-wise consciousness of Hermes, Pan, and especially Dionysus.

Whereas the myths we referred to earlier depicted a masculine deity removed from the plight of the feminine, stationary and fixed, the fluid and passionate nature of Dionysus, the fact that he changes easily from one form to another and that he is specifically a god of the feminine, suggests another way out of the dilemma of an ego-consciousness too far removed from the soul. In much of the same way that the appearance of the cult of Dionysus in Greek culture signalled the independence of women from the Demeter-like role of mother, wife, sister to man, so too may the arrival of a Dionystic stance on the shore of our psychic awareness free anima from earth, release Athena from Daddy.

James Hillman had alerted us to the idea that the way "to another consciousness thus begins by taking back those feminine aspects of the primal union, by returning to our own primary bisexuality."[85] By accepting the feminine, by doing more than observing her plight from the height of our intellectual note-taking and head-shaking, and by recognizing that the physiological qualities we have deemed inferior are actually projections of our own psychological interiority, we can restore our path to the androgyne.[86]

The mere conscious acceptance of the anima as idea however will not be enough. The activation of the androgyne calls for a fusion, a mingling of opposites into one permanent body. And this cannot be done without the freeing of anima first through a ritual immersion in anima, through methods that free up the waters of our imagination. Whether this will indeed lead to the creation of a yoga is to be seen.

My reflections have concerned themselves with what is eternal in all of us, the soul of our humanity without which the androgyne is a fiction.

NOTES

[1]"It is a remarkable fact that perhaps the majority of cosmogonic gods are of a bisexual nature. The hermaphrodite means nothing less than a union of the strongest and most striking opposites. In the first place this union refers back to a primitive state of mind, a twilight where differences and contrasts were either barely separated or completely merged. With increasing clarity of consciousness, however, the opposites draw more and more distinctly and irreconcilably apart." *Essays on a Science of Mythology*, C. G. Jung and C. Kerenyi, Harper Torchbooks, New York, 1963, p. 92.

[2]C. G. Jung, *CW* 9 (i) par. 512.

[3]"The splitting of the Original Man into husband and wife expresses an act of nascent consciousness; it gives birth to a pair of opposites, thereby making consciousness possible." Jung, *CW* 9 (ii), para. 320. Also see Maria von Franz, *Creation Myths*, Spring Publications, second unrevised printing, New York/Zurich, p. 155.

[4]Jung, *CW* 13, par. 456.

[5]"Mercurius is likened to the 'matrimonium' or coniunctio; that is to say he *is* the marriage on account of his androgynous form." Jung, *CW* 14, par. 12, p. 17.

[6]*C. G. Jung: Letters*, Gerhard Adler/Aniela Jaffe, editors, Princeton University Press, Princeton, New Jersey, 1975, vol. II, p. 394.

[7]Jung, *CW* 9 (i), par. 519.

[8]"The roles which Jung . . . assigns to the anima . . . all appear frequently and validly in the psychology of women. Anima phenomenology is not restricted to the male sex. . . The intensifications, exaggerations, and mythologizings that belong to the description of the anima do appear in women and may not be ascribed to her unconscious feminine personality, the woman within, or attributed to a minority of female genes." "Anima" by James Hillman, *Spring 1973*, Spring Publications, New York, p. 115.

⁹*ibid.*, pp. 114ff.

¹⁰cf. note 4 above and *Letters*, vol. II, *op. cit.*, p. 395.

¹¹Jung, *CW*, 11, par. 268.

¹²Jung, *CW*, 8, par. 439.

¹³*ibid.*, par. 964. Also see, *C. G. Jung: Letters*, Princeton University Press, Princeton, N.J., 1973, vol. I, p. 433.

¹⁴"Synchronicity therefore means the simultaneous concurrence of a certain psychic state with one or more external events which appear as meaningful parallels to the momentary subjective state — and, in certain cases, vice versa." Jung, *CW*, 8, par. 850. Also, "certain phenomena of simultaneity or synchronicity seem to be bound up with the archetypes." *ibid.*, par. 841.

¹⁵"*Mundus Imaginalis* or the Imaginary and the Imaginal," by Henry Corbin, in *Spring 1972*, Analytical Psychology Club of New York, p. 10. Corbin's elucidation of the spiritual world of the Sufi corresponds with Jung's in that he too thought of the archetypes as existing independently of one another while at the same time being contained in one another. cf. *CW* 11, par. 440; also von Franz, *op. cit.* Lecture I, p. 10.

¹⁶Thus, the "work" on the androgyne demands the altruistic attitude of the early alchemist: "For the alchemist, the one primarily in need of redemption is not man, but the deity who is lost and sleeping in matter. Only as a secondary consideration does he hope that some benefit may accrue to himself from the transformed substance as the panacea, the *medicina catholica*. . . His attention is not directed to his own salvation through God's grace, but to the liberation of God from the darkness of matter. By applying himself to this miraculous work he benefits from its salutary effect, but only incidentally. He may approach the work as one in need of salvation, but he knows that his salvation depends on the success of the work, on whether he can free the divine soul." Jung, *CW* 12 (second edition, 1968), par. 420.

¹⁷*The Logos of the Soul*, Evangelos Christou, Dunquin Press, Vienna/Zurich, 1963, p. 102.

¹⁸*The Varieties of Religious Experience*, William James, Longmans, Green and Co., New York, 1910, p. 388.

On the Androgyne

[19]*ibid.*, p. 516.

[20]"Therefore they determined the tao of heaven and called it the dark and the light. They determined the tao of the earth and called it the yielding and the firm. They determined the tao of man and called it love and rectitude." *The I Ching or Book of Changes*, Wilhelm/Baynes, trans., Princeton University Press, third edition, 1973, p. 264.

[21]"As opposites never unite at their own level . . . a supraordinate 'Third' is always required, in which the two parts can come together." Jung, *CW*, 9 (ii), par. 280.

[22]*Creative Imagination in the Sufism of Ibn'Arabi*, Henry Corbin, Princeton University Press, Princeton, N.J., 1969, p. 80. Jung expressed this idea early in his career: "This aim of totality can be recognized neither by the science, whose end is in itself, nor by feeling, which lacks the faculty of vision belonging to thought. The one must lend itself as auxillary to the other, yet the contrast between them is so great that we need a bridge. This bridge is already given us in creative phantasy." *Psychological Types*, C. G. Jung, Harcourt, Brace & Co., Inc., New York, 1923, p. 77.

The transformative power of phantasy, later called active imagination, was a powerful issue in Jung's mind, *vide*: "All the difficulties you overcome in such a fantasy are symbolic expressions of psychological difficulties in yourself, and inasmuch as you overcome them in your imagination you also overcome them in your psyche." *Letters*, vol. I, *op. cit.*, p. 109.

[23]Jung, *CW* 11, par. 889.

[25]*Kama-Kala-Vilasa*, Sir John Woodroffe, trans., Ganesh & Co., Madras, third edition, 1961, p. 6.

[25]"Thou are neither girl, nor maid, nor old. Indeed, thou are neither female nor male, nor neuter. Thou art inconceivable, immeasurable Power, the Being of all which exists, void of all duality, the Supreme Brahman, attainable in Illumination alone." From the *Mahakala-Samhita*, quoted in *S'akti and S'akta*, by Sir John Woodroffe, Ganesh & Co., Madras, sixth edition, 1965, p. 28.

[26]*ibid.*, p. 39.

[27]*The Serpent Power*, Sir John Woodroffe, Ganesh & Co., Madras, seventh edition, 1964, p. 41.

[28]*Introduction to Tantra Shastra*, Sir John Woodruffe, Ganesh & Co., Madras, second edition, 1952, p. 34.

[29]Briefly described, the system of the chakras in the human body is as follows:

The first chakra, *Muladhara* ("the root base"), is located midway between the genitals above and the anus below. Each chakra is given the image of the lotus, and the color of this lotus is crimson. It is square and its element is earth. It is here that the Kundalini in the form of a serpent coiled three times around the Divine Lingam or phallus, slumbers. This latter scene is found in the middle of a yellow triangle identified as the Yoni, or female genitals.

The second chakra, *Svadhisthana* (abode of Shakti), is located at the root of the genitals and within the *Susumna nadi*. The *nadi* is a channel, of which there are three. The *Susumna nadi* goes straight up the center of the spine. The *Ida nadi* is situated to the left of this *nadi* and the *Pingala nadi* is situated to the right. These two latter channels intertwine the central channel, both of them originating in the first chakra and both meeting in the fifth (ajna) chakra. The *Ida nadi* culminates in the left nostril, the *Pingala* in the right. The *Ida* is also known as the moon, the *Pingala* as the sun. This second chakra is the first to be located within the central channel. The first (Muladhara) is imagined as immediately at the base of the Susumna, the mouth of the slumbering Kundalini engulfing its base. The color of this lotus is vermilion and its element is water.

The third chakra, *Manipura* ("the city of the lustrous gem"), is located in the navel region. Its color is blue and its element is fire.

The fourth chakra, *Anahata* ("the sound which comes without the striking of any two things together"), is located at the level of the heart. Its color is ruddy and its element is air.

The fifth chakra, *Visuddha* ("completely purified"), is located at the base of the throat. Its color is a smoky purple and its element is ether.

The sixth chakra, *Ajna* ("Lotus of Command"), is located between the two eye-brows. Its color is white and it is imagined as existing beyond the zones of the five elements.

Above this last chakra is *Sahasrara* ("the lotus of a thousand petals"), in which Para-siva awaits the return of and conjunction with his Shakti, Kundalini.

The first three chakras (*Muladhara, Svadhisthana*, and *Manipura*) comprise the gross body, the last three the subtle.

The description of the chakras has been culled from *Kundalini Yoga* by M. P. Pandit, Ganesh & Co., Madras, second edition, 1962, p. 32ff. The translation of the chakra titles are from Heinrich Zimmer's "The Chakras of Kundalini Yoga," in *Spring 1975*, pp. 33ff.

On the Androgyne   121

[30]cf. *The Serpent Power, op. cit.*, p. 228.

[31]The danger is that the aroused serpent-power might enter either the ida or the pingala, the result of which is disastrous. For a gruelling account of such a mishap I refer the reader to *Kundalini: The Evolutionary Energy in Man*, Gopi Krishna, Shambhala, Berkeley, 1971. Also see "On the Significance of the Indian Tantric Yoga," by Heinrich Zimmer, *Spiritual Disciplines*, edited by Joseph Campbell, Pantheon Books, New York, 1960.

[32]*The Yoga Upanishad*, T. R. Srinivasa Ayyangar, trans., The Adyar Library, Madras, 1952.

[33]cf. *The Serpent Power, op. cit.*, pp. 31ff.

[34] Jung, *CW*, 8, par. 246.

[35]*ibid.*, par. 243.

[36]Here, and in the greater portion of references to Jung's statements concerning the anima as the archetype of reflection and consciousness, I am indebted to James Hillman's research contained in his "Anima," (I & II), *Spring 1973, Spring 1974*.

[37]Jung, *CW*, 11, par. 240, quoted in Hillman, *ibid.*, 1973, p. 125.

[38]*ibid.*

[39]*ibid.*, pp. 125-6.

[40]*ibid.*, p. 126.

[41]cf. *Kundalini Yoga, op. cit.*, pp. 40ff.

[42]Jung, *CW* 14, par. 129.

[43]Jung, *CW* 11, par. 252.

[44]*Gnosticism and Early Christianity*, Robert M. Grant, Harper Torchbooks, New York, 1966, pp. 19ff.

[45]*ibid.* pp. 76, 77.

[46]Jung, *CW*, 13, par. 454.

[47] *ibid.*, par. 457.

[48] *ibid.*, par. 455.

[49] Jung's ideas on the muladhara and svadhisthana chakras are culled from Lectures I & II of his "Psychological Commentary on Kundalini Yoga," published in *Spring 1975*.

[50] *ibid.* p. 11.

[51] *ibid.*, p. 15.

[52] *ibid.*, p. 9.

[53] ". . . we begin in our conscious world, so our *muladhara* might be, not down below in the belly, but up in the head. . . In the East the unconscious is above, while with us it is below, so we can reverse the whole thing, as if we were coming down from *muladhara*, as if that were the highest centre." *ibid.*, p. 12.

[54] I must now alert the reader that I take leave of Jung's commentary on the Kundalini, becoming fully responsible for what follows.

[55] *The Discovery of the Unconscious*, Henri F. Ellenberger, Basic Books, New York, 1970, pp. 518ff.

[56] ". . . mental productions are regularly present in all the psychoneuroses . . . and these . . . phantasies have important connections with the causes of the neurotic symptoms." "Hysterical Phantasies and their Relations to Bisexuality," in *Sigmund Freud: Collected Papers*, Basic Books, New York, 1959, vol. II, p. 51.

[57] *ibid.*, p. 53.

[58] *ibid.*, p. 57. While Freud makes this statement solely in relation to the symptoms of hysteria, his opening argument that all neurotic symptoms display phantasy production generalizes his observation.

[59] "The Theory of the Instincts," in *An Outline of Psychoanalysis*, Clara Thompson, editor, Modern Library, New York, 1955, p. 6.

[60] *ibid.*, p. 7.

[61] *ibid.*, p. 6.

[62]*ibid.*, p. 8.

[63]*ibid.*

[64]"The Development of the Sexual Function," *ibid.*, pp. 9-13.

[65]*ibid.*, p. 11.

[66]I am indebted here to Dr. James Hillman's *The Myth of Analysis*, Northwestern University Press, Evanston, Ill., 1972, p. 242, for bringing this information to my attention.

[67]"Whenever a psychological theory is forcibly applied, we have reason to suspect an archetypal fantasy-image is trying to distort reality . . ." Jung, *CW*, 9 (i), p. 69n.

[68]*The Sacred and the Profane: The Nature of Religion*, Mircea Eliade, Harcourt, Brace & World, New York, 1959, p. 13.

[69]"The spiritual development of the West has been along entirely different lines from that of the East and has therefore produced conditions which are the most unfavorable soil one can think of for the application of yoga." Jung, *CW*, 11, par. 876. Also see, "The Realities of Practical Psychotherapy," *CW*, 16, second edition.

[70]Jung, *CW*, 11, par. 876, 873.

[71]cf. *Freud and the Post-Freudians*, J. A. C. Brown, Penguin Books, Baltimore, 1961, p. 29.

[72]cf. Hillman, "Anima" (I), *op. cit.*, p. 117: "The *per definitionem* absence of anima in women is a deprivation of a cosmic principle with no less consequence in the practice of analytical psychology than has been the theory of penis deprivation in the practice of psychoanalysis."

[73]*The Homeric Gods*, Walter F. Otto, Beacon Press, Boston, 1954, p. 53.

[74]Adapted from Zimmer's recounting of the tale in *Myths and Symbols in Indian Art and Civilization*, Heinrich Zimmer, Harper Torchbooks, New YHork, 1962, pp. 128ff.

[75]*ibid.*, p. 129.

[76]*ibid.*, p. 127.

[77]Otto, *op. cit.*, p. 104.

[78]*Pan and the Nightmare: Two Essays*, Wilhelm Heinrich Roscher, James Hillman, Spring Publications, Zurich, Switzerland, 1972, pp. xxvii.

[79]*Sexual Symbolism: A History of Phallic Worship*, Richard Payne Knight, Thomas Wright, Bell Publishing Co., New York, reprint, mcmlvii, p. 29.

[80]*Dionysus: Myth and Cult*, Walter F. Otto, Indiana University Press, Bloomington and London, 1955, p. 164.

[81]*Ancient Incubation Theory and Modern Psychotherapy*, C. A. Meier, Northwestern University Press, Evanston, Ill., 1967, p. 65.

[82]*ibid.*, p. 63.

[83]*The Greeks and their Gods*, W. K. C. Guthrie, Beacon Press, Boston, fourth printing, 1962, pp. 106ff.

[84]*The Meridian Handbook of Classical Mythology*, Edward Tripp, Meridian, New York, 1970, p. 118.

[85]*The Myth of Analysis*, James Hillman, Northwestern University Press, Evanston, Ill, 1972, p. 282.

[86]"The *physiological* qualities which have been declared inferior and to belong to the female would now become *psychological* qualities appropriate to man or woman. Inferiority would no longer be only feminine, because we now see it as part of a conjoined human consciousness; and the feminine would no longer be inferior, because it belongs to this structure of generally human consciousness." *ibid.*, p. 282.

INDEX

"A Child is Being Beaten" (Freud), 55 n.6
Accident, as wound, 24
Adam, 59, 60, 61, 63, 64, 65, 67, 78, 81; as ego, 62, 63; as hermaphrodite, 59, 63; image of God, 63; second, 70; suicide of 62; symbolic of God's problem, 69
Afterlife, 25, 26
Ajna, 113, 115, 120 n. 29
Akropolis, 115
Alchemists, 7, 12, 15, 16, 26, 44, 60, 79, 80, 88, 118 n. 16
Alchemy, 15, 16, 18, 29, 31, 41; the couple in, 74; and the soul's imagination, 18; and tria prima theory, 15; as yoga, 88
Alexander the Great, as serpent, 115
Amnesia, post-hypnotic, 107
Amor and Psyche, 50
Anahata, 120 n. 29
Ancient Incubation Theory and Modern Psychotherapy, (Meier), 124, n. 81
Androgyne, 75, 92, 96, 97, 105, 107, 110, 116, 118 n. 16; activation of, 96; and archetypal, 93; as Christ, 60, 70, 93, 110; as a consciousness, 96, 113; and feminine, 101; geography of, 95; as God, 61; as marriage of opposites, 64; as Mercurius, 95, 117; and neurosis, 108; preexistent, 95; as realization, 93; as subtle body, 93; and transpersonal reality, 95; world of, 98
"An Essay on Pan" (Hillman), 55 n. 20
Anima, 106, 112, 117 n. 8, 123 n. 72; and animus, 92, 93, 94, 95, 97, 102, 105, 108, 116; as connecting link, 104; and ego, 94; imagining, 107; and men, 94, 104; and neurosis, 108; and reflection, 113; rejection of, 105; as shadow in women, 94; and women, 94
"Anima" I & II, (Hillman), 117 n. 8; 121 n. 36; 123 n. 72
Anima Mundi, 39; and philosopher's stone, 41; exists in the imaginal, 42
Animus, & anima, 92, 93, 94, 95, 97, 105, 108; and women, 94; & neurosis, 108
An Outline of Psychoanalysis, 108
Aphrodite, 51; beasts accompany, 49; & castration, 48, 49; & compulsion, 50; mistress of Ares, 49; mother of fear & terror, 49; murderous passion of, 49; psyche ridden by, 49, 50; & Virgin Mary, 49
Archei, 15
Archetype/archetypal, 7, 18, 39, 40, 44, 71, 79, 82, 96, 97, 99, 109, 110, 111, 118 n. 15; activation of, 96; active imagination, 44; & body, 22; connections, 42; definition of, 30; & ego, 95; & feminine, 79; hero-, 95; & horoscope, 40, 43, 47; humanizing of, 39; imagining, 53; of inferiority, 80; & Kronus, 36; -language, 31; life, 31; matter, 79; meaning, 43; & Mercurius, 95; mother-, 95; phantasy-image, 123 n. 67; Philosopher's Stone, 41; psychological, 31; seeing, 31; soul, not property of, 39; & synchronicity, 118; -wholeness, 40, 43, 47; & transformative process, 110; & zodiac, 41, 43
Archeus, 13
Ares, see Mars
Aristotle, element theory of, 14
Ashmole, Elias, 41
Asiyah, 104
Asklepios, as serpent, 115
Astrology, 19, 20, 21, 26, 37, 38, 39, 40, 42, 43, 47; as counselling, 31; danger for, 54; & four element theory, 14, 26; natal chart, 40; & wholeness, 41, 43
Athena, 112, 113, 116; & serpent, 115
Atlas, 53
Augustus, as serpent, 115
Avicenna, 12
Avidya, as earth, 88
Ayyangar, T.R. Srinivasa, 121n. 31

Bacchus, 114
Barnes, Djuna, 87
Bios, & soul, 58
Bloom, Leopold, 97
Body, 22, 25, 80, 84, 94, 104, 11, 113; & archetypal, 22; as earth, 100; & ego, 41; as erotegenic zone, 108; four humours of, 15; & Gods, 22; healed, 20; as hermaphrodite, 93; & illness, 15; imaginal, 110; & psyche, 23; & sefiroth, 60; & soul, 15, 80, 92; & sulpher-mercury, 15; a temple, 26; transpersonal, 110
Body, subtle, 20, 25; as androgyne, 93, 95; not created, 26; creation of, 47; & death, 41; as Philospher's Stone, 42; & wholeness, 41; world of, 101
Bombast, Georg, 11
Bone, eternal & divine, 63; as feminine principle, 63
Book of Adam & Eve, 62
Brahma, 113, 114
Brown, J.A.C., 123 n. 71
Buddha, 24

Calendar, seasonal & astronomical, 32ff
Campbell, Joseph, 121 n. 31
Casey, Edward S. 55 n. 21
Castration, 36; and Aprhrodite, 48; and ego, 36
Celsus, 12
Chakra(s), 100, 102, 105, 109, 112, 113, 115, 120 n. 29; inverted in West, 106
"The Chakras of Kundalini Yoga," 120 n. 29
Chavvah, 77
Chayyah, 77
Chemistry, 13, 18
China, 77
Christ, 24; as androgyne, 60, 70, 93, 110; God as, 70; imitation of, 23; as Philosopher's Stone, 60
Christianity, 60, 111
Christou, Evangelous, 96, 118 n. 17
Complex, ego as, 41; mother-father, 41; as a personality, 41
Compulsion, & Aphrodite, 50; & Kronos, 49; & sexuality, 48; of Uranos, 51; value in, 49
Conjunction, with the feminine, 84
Consciousness, 33, 39, 42, 44, 46, 52, 53, 67, 69, 94, 97, 98, 99, 100, 105, 111, 112, 117, 122 n. 53, 124 n. 86; & androgyne, 93, 96, 99, 113; controls, 24; as desert, 63; differentiated, 93; divinity of, 61; ego, 42, 63, 95; extension of, 87; extinction of, 93; hermaphrodite as symbolic of, 59, 92, 93; & image, 98; Kronian, 47; & libido, 44; limit of, 52; as masculine, 33, 34, 103; & opposites, 61, 64, 92, 93, 117; personified in myth, 32; & reflec-

tion, 102, 121 n. 36; Saturn &, 36, 37, 52; as serpent, 64, 65; & separation, 92; & Shiva-Shakti, 101, 111; as sin, 62; & Sol/sun, 35, 92; solar and lunar, 71, 88; soul won by, 63; & suffering, 70; & synchronicity, 96; Uranian, 47
Copernicus, 16
Corbin, Henri, 30, 54 n. 2, 96, 98, 118 n. 15, 119 n. 22
Corpus Hermeticum (Scott), 56 n. 23
Counselling, 39, 40, 43, 45; dangers of Saturnian, 47; & Saturn, 31, 49
Creation, 92; grossest part of, 76; Hindu, 66, 77; imagination &, 67; myths & neurosis, 108; seven days of, 71; Winnebago myth, 65ff
Creation Myths, (von Franz), 117
Creative Imagination in the Sufism of Ibn 'Arabi (Corbin), 119 n. 22
The Crow, 85
Cupid, 108
Cure, 22
Cyclopes, 32

Daemons, 16
Death/dying, 25; denial of, 25; & Nature, 26; as process, 25; & skeleton, 63; & soul, 48, 53; & subtle body, 41; Tree of Knowledge &, 64; & water, 48
Deimos, & Aphrodite, 49
Delos, 114
Demeter, 32
Depression, function of Saturn, 48
Desert, as consciousness, 63; & soul, 63
"The Development of the Sexual Function" (Freud), 123 n. 64
"The Devouring Father" (Stein), 55 n. 11
Dionysus, 115, 116; & phallus, 114
Dionysus: Myth & Cult (Otto), 124 n. 80
The Discovery of the Unconscious (Ellenberger), 122 n. 55
Disease, 23, 25; aestheticism of, 21; & Gods, 22, 23; Paracelsus' theory of, 13, 15
Dissolution, of Nature, 26
"The Dream and the Underworld" (Hillman), 54 n. 3

Earth, 84; as chakra, 106; body &, 80, 100; as female, 33, 104; feminine housed in, 105; as Great Mother, 33; as ignorance, 88; as Kabbalistic Kingdom, 76; life is, 48; as Malkuth, 76; soul trapped on, 63; water & 48
Eden, 62, 69; wife of Elohim, 103
Ego, 37, 42, 46, 87, 104, 111, 112; Adam as, 62, 63; angelology of, 26; & archetype, 95; & castration, 36; as complex, 41, 42; & consciousness, 41, 63, 95, 97; differentiation of, 63; diminutive, 62; dry, 48; -world, 99; as idealized center, 42; & Kronus &, 34; & libido, 108; male, 94; as masculine, 34; & Paradise, 63; primitive aspects of, 46; & reflection, 102; & self,112; & Shiva, 103; subtle body, 41; young, 62
Elements, & astrology, 26; four humours & tempers of, 14; soul of, 15
Eliade, Mircea, 71, 110, 123 n. 68
Elohim, creator of universe, 103; husband of Eden, 103
Ellenberger, Henri F., 122 n. 55

Embryogenesis (Grossinger), 7
Empiricism, 39
Eros, 38, 109, 114; compulsion & 51; as Freudian libido, 108; & moon, 101; in muladhara, 108; & psyche, 49, 50
Erotogenic, zones, 108, 109
Essays on a Science of Mythology, (Jung/Kerenyi), 117
Eve, 59, 61, 62, 64, 76, 78, 81; & consciousness, 65; & serpent, 61; as soul, 63
Exhalations, 15

Fairytales, 85, 86
Father, as heaven, 60; and hermaphrodite, 60
Female, 59, 88, 94, 111; as counterpart, 75; earth as, 53; psyche as, 85; rejection of, 105
Feminine, 33 ff, 59, 60, 63, 78ff, 80, 83, 84, 87, 88, 105, 106, 111, 112, 116, 124 n. 86; androgyne &, 101; as bone, 63; conjunction with, 84; debased, 78; divine, 77; & earth, 77, 104, 105; exalted, 75; exiled, 76, 80; existence &, 79; inferior, 60, 110; Kronos limits, 49; & masculine, 86, 93; & matter 79, 80; & men, 33, 34, 86; prisoner, 77; queenly aspects of, 84; reflective, 112, 113; rejected, 79; relationship to, 74; shakti, 95; as soul, 63; & transformation, 81; unconscious as, 103
Freeman, Kathleen, 56 n. 25 & 31
Freud & the Post-Freudians (Brown), 123 n. 71
Freud, Sigmund, 33, 34, 36, 55 n. 6, 80, 108, 109, 110, 112, 122 n. 56, 58, 123 n. 71; & hypnosis, 107; & imagination, 107; & myth of the unconscious, 107
From Primitives to Zen (Eliade) 71 n. 3 & 4

Gaia, 32
Galen, 12, 14, 15
Galenic theory, 15
Galileo, 16
The Game of Wizards: Psyche, Science, & Symbolism in the Occult (Poncé), p. 54 n. 5
Genesis, 59, 66, 68, 69; continuance of, 47; God of, 61, 65; & hermaphrodite, 93; second, 62; the work of, 45
Genitals, 76, 93, 106, 109, 110, 113; & unconscious, 106
The Glass Axe, 83
Gnosticism, of Simon, 104; & Sophia, 104; of Justin, 103
Gnosticism & Early Christianity (Grant), 121 n. 44
God(s) 74, 111; Adam as image of, 63; androgynous, 61; apprehension of, 45; of astrology, 38; Christ as, 70; & disease, 22, 23, 47, 64; in evolution, 45; & feminine, 76; of Genesis, 61, 65; Hermaphrodite created by, 61; & imagination, 67; individuation of, 45; loneliness of, 65ff; & opposites, 68; as psychic factors, 30; image of self, 63; & serpent, 65; unconscious, 67, 68; unity of, 68; wounded, 23
Gold, 29; found in filth, 79
Grant, Robert M., 121 n. 44
Greeks, 16
The Greeks & their Gods (Guthrie), 124 n. 83
Grossinger, Richard, 7
Guthrie, W.K.C., 124 n. 83

Hades, 32, 53, 54
Hartmann, Franz, 27 n. 1 & 3
Heart, emotion & intuition of, 63

Head, contains Shiva, 103
Heaven, as father, 60; & hermaphrodite, 60; imagination &, 41, 42, 46; & lead of, 52; of Paracelsus, 46; of the soul, 52
Hephaestus, 49
Hera, 32
Heraclitus, 48, 52, 53, 58
Hermaphrodite, 92, 99, 117; Adam as, 59, 93; asexual, 60; as body, 93; in Christianity, 60; God created, 61; in Judaism, 60; as Mercurius, 95; & neurosis, 108; & opposites, 60; Paradise of, 98; transformation of, 95; unconscious, 61, 64, 92, 93; undivided, 92
Hermes, 116; & phallus, 114; & unconscious, 114; & underworld, 114
The Hermetic & Alchemical Writings of Paracelsus, 27 n. 2 & 6, 55 n. 12
Hermetica (Scott), 45
Hermetic Museum (Waite), 89
Hesiod, 32, 48, 49, 52, 53
Hestia, 32
Hiranyagarbha, 100
Hillman, James, 43, 44, 46, 53, 54 n. 3, 55 n. 16, 55 n. 20, 62, 71 n. 1, 82, 89 n. 2, 94, 95, 114, 116, 117 n. 18, 121 n. 36 & 37, 123 n. 66 & 72, 124 n. 78 & 85
History, Kronus as archetype of, 36
The Homeric Gods (Otto), 123 n. 73
Horoscope, 45, 46; as active imagination of Gods, 45; & archetypal imagination, 45; & archetypal wholeness, 40; the imaginal, 42; soul's expression of itself, 26
Humours, four, 14; & body, 15; governed by planets, 15; Paracelsus' theory of, 15
Hypnosis, & amnesia, 107; & Freud, 107
"Hysterical Phantasies & their Relations to Bisexuality" (Freud), 122 n. 56

Iatrochemists & iatrochemistry, 15, 16
Ibn 'Arabi, 58
Ida, 101, 120 n. 29, 121 n. 31
The I Ching or Book of Changes (Wilhelm/Baynes), 119 n. 20
Illness, 15, 18, 23; & God, 22, 47; mental, 13; metaphors of, 23
Image, concretized, 62; & consciousness, 44, 98; of God, 63; of the horoscope, 45; & libido, 144; & myth, 38, 39; & sleep, 53; of the soul, 75; transformation of, 44, 58
Imaginal, 17, 18, 45, 47, 52, 74, 106, 107; & androgyne, 99; dimension, 43; horoscope, 42; & imagination, 42; of Paracelsus, 46; & pathology, 99; - & transpersonal body, 111; work, 43
Imagination, 17, 18, 20, 40, 59, 106, 111; active, 44, 45, 67, 119 n. 22; archetypal, 44, 46, 53; astrology born of, 20; Creation, 67; & Freud, 107; & the Gods, 38; heaven created by, 42; & horoscope, 45, 46; imaginal composed of, 42; organ of, 98; & Philosopher's Stone, 41; & soul, 26, 43; & transformation, 58; world created by 101; & yoga, 101
Individuation, of the Gods, 45
Initiation, 83
Instinct(s), 83, 102; & compulsion, 44; in Freudian psychology, 108; in Jungian psychology, 101; & Kronos, 49; reflective, 102; as serpent, 65; value in, 49

Introduction to Tantra Shastra (Woodroffe), 120 n. 28
Ishshah, 77

Jabir ibn Hayyan, 14, 15
James, William, 97, 118 n. 18
Joyce, James, 96
Judaism, 60
Jung, Carl, 22, 23, 24, 27 n. 5, 30, 35, 37, 38, 39, 41, 42, 44, 47, 53, 54 n. 1 & 4, 55 n. 8-10, 15, 19 & 22, 56 n. 24, 28 & 29, 71 n. 2, 92, 93, 94, 95, 96, 98, 101, 102, 104, 105, 106, 111, 112, 115, 117 n. 1-8, 118 n. 11-16, 119 n. 21, 22, & 23, 121 n. 34, 36, 37, 42, 43, & 46, 122 n. 49 & 54, 123 n. 67, 69, & 70
Collected Letters of, 117 n. 6, 118 n. 13, 119 n. 22
Collected Works of, 27 n. 5, 54 n. 1 & 4, 55 n. 8-10, 15, 19, & 22, 56 n. 28 & 29, 71 n. 2, 117 n. 2-5 & 7, 118 n. 11-12, & 14-16, 119 n. 21 & 23, 121 n. 34, 37, 42, 43 & 46, 123 n. 67, 69 & 70
Justin, Gnosticism of 103

Kabbalism, 60, 75, 105, 110; four world of, 104
Kalpana, 101
Kama, 100
Kama-Kala-Vilasa (Woodroffe), 76, 119 n. 25
Kellipoth, 76
Kerenyi, Karl, 82, 89 n. 1, 117
Kether, & soul, 76
Knight, Richard Payne, 124 n. 79
Krishna, Gopi, 121 n. 31
Kronos, see Saturn
Kundalini, 103, 104, 105, 112, 113, 115, 120 n. 29, 121 n. 31, 122 n. 54; & lingam, 61, 106; & serpent of Genesis, 64; as Shakti, 100; -yoga, 95
Kundalini: The Evolutionary Energy in Man (Krishna), 121 n. 31
Kundalini Yoga (Pandit), 120 n. 29, 121 n. 41

Lead, alchemical 29; key of heaven, 52, resolves imperfections, 52; Saturn as synonym for, 29
Leibniz, 74
Libido, 108, 109; apprehended by the image, 44; & ego, 108; as Eros, 108; Freudian theory of, 108
Lindsay, Jack, 56 n. 27
Logos, & sun, 101
Lingam, 120 n. 29, & kundalini, 61
Loneliness, God's, 65ff; Shiva &, 77
The Logos of the Soul (Christou), 118 n. 17
Love, & Aphrodite, 49; born of castration, 48; & Kronian blindness, 49
Lucretius, 49
Luna, 78; as unconscious, 35

Macrocosm, 100
Mahabramanda, 100
Male, 59, 86, 88, 94; ego, 94; as Great Father, 33; psyche, 85; as sky, 33
Malkuth, as earth, 76; as Kingdom, 76
Mana, skeleton as -object, 63
Manipura, 120 n. 29
Marriage, Sacred, & Mercurius, 95, 117; of the sun and moon, 71

Mars, 19; & Aphrodite, 49
Masculine, 35ff, 59, 60, 85, 87, 88, 106, 116; & Athena, 113; consciousness as, 33, 103; & feminine, 86, 93; fixity of, 104; reconciliation with, 84; & reflection, 113; serpent as, 115; as spirit, 81; superiority, 74, 110; tyrannical, 60; & unconscious, 33; & yang, 95
Matter, 80; is feminine, 79, 80; & Uranos, 47
Medicine, 15, 18, 26
Medusa, 113
Meier, C.A., 124 n. 81
Meister Eckhart, 52
Mercurius, as androgyne, 95; as archetypal reality, 95; as collective unconscious, 95; as conjunction, 117; as hermaphrodite, 95; sacred marriage occurs in, 95
The Meridian Handbook of Greek Mythology (Tripp), 124 n. 84
Mercury, treatment for syphilis, 12
Meru, Mt. 100
Metis, 32, 37, 112; aspect of soul, 52
Microcosm, 100
Mind, healed by heavens, 20
Moon, -channel, 101
Mother, 84; as earth, 60; & hermaphrodite, 60
Mother, Great, myths of and calendar, 32; as personification, 33
Muladhara, 100, 105, 112, 113, 120 n. 29, 122 n. 49 & 53; as earth 106; contains eros, 108
"Mundus Imaginalis or the Imaginary & the Imaginal" (Corbin), 54 n. 2, 118 n. 15
The Myth of Analysis (Hillman), 123 n. 66, 124 n. 85
Myth/mythology, 38ff, 83, 112; Freudian, 110; Horoscope as continuation of, 45; & psychology, 30; of unconscious, 107
Myths and Symbols in Indian Art and Civilization (Zimmer), 123 n. 74

Natal chart, 40
Nature 25, 82; & archetypes, 39; & death, 26; dissolution of, 26; spirit in, 64; untamed, 102; the work of, 44
Neumann, Erich, 34, 55 n. 7
Neurosis, 108, 122 n. 58; positive, 22; symptoms, 122 n. 56
Nightwood (Barnes), 87
Nu-chieh, 77

Oceanus, 52, 112
Ochsner, Elsa, 11
Oedipus, 36, 110
"On the Significance of the Indian Tantric Yoga" (Zimmer), 121 n. 31
Opposites, 23, 46, 61, 71, 75, 111, 119 n. 21; androgyne as marriage of, 64; in China, 76ff; conflict of, 70; & consciousness, 93; God composed of, 68; & hermaphrodite, 60, 93; & human condition, 61; reconciliation of, 106
Olympus, 46
On the Nature of Things (Lucretius), 49
Organs, 21; soul expressed through, 26
The Origins & History of Consciousness (Neumann), 55 n. 7
The Origins of Alchemy in Graeco-Roman Egypt (Lindsay), 56 n. 27
Orpheus, 114

Osiris, 114
Otto, Walter, 113, 123 n. 73, 124 n. 77 & 80
An Outline Of Psychoanalysis (Freud), 122 n. 59

Pan, 38, 115, 116; & phallus, 114
Pan & the Nightmare, Two Essays (Hillman), 55 n. 20, 124 n. 78
Pandit, M.P., 120 n. 29
Paracelsus, 16, 17, 18, 20, 21, 26, 27 n. 1 & 2, 40, 42, 43, 55 n. 12, 55 n. 14; birth and death of, 11; chemical theory of humours, 15
Paracelsus: Life & Prophecies (Hartmann) 27 n. 1
Paradise, 63, 64, 70; ego and, 63; of Genesis, 59; of hermaphrodite, 68; as unconscious, 62, 63
Parashiva 100, 112; as sun, 100
Pathology, & imaginal, 99
Perseus, 113
Phallus, 113, 120 n. 29; Greek Gods of, 114; & Kundalini 106, 109
Pharmaceutics/pharmacology, 13, 16, 18
Philosopher's Stone, as androgyne, 60; as Christ, 60, 71; as subtle body, 42; & zodiacal archetype, 41
Phobos, & Aphrodite, 49
Pingala, 101 120 n. 29, 121 n. 31
Plato, 53, 56 n. 30
Plutarch, 114
The Collected Dialogues of Plato, 56 n. 30
Poimandres of Hermes Trismegistus, 80
Planets, 20; & alchemy, 15; four humours of, 15; as Gods, 38
Polarities, see opposites
Poncé, Charles, 54 n. 5
Poseidon, 32
The Pre-Socratic Philosophers (Freeman) 56 n. 25
Prince, 85
Princess, 85
Projection, 34, 70, 97, 116; & consciousness, 35; of inferiority, 80; of our souls, 75; withdrawl, 98
Psyche, 17, 21, 33, 35, 37, 43, 50, 84, 96, 113; & Aphrodite, 49; archetypes transcend, 38; & body, 23, 92; & Eros, 49; evolutionary, 111; God's, 65, 70; of the infant, 61; & inferiority, 80; male, 85; & reflection, 102
Psychic energy, see Libido
"Psychological Commentary on Kundalini Yoga" (Jung), 122 n. 49
Psychology, 18, 21, 37, 40, 43; & imaginal, 99, 111; & mythology, 30; personification in, 35; separates person from cosmos, 39
Psychological Types (Jung), 119 n. 22
Purusha, 66, 100
Putrefactio, 26

Queen, 83, 84

"The Realities of Practical Psychotherapy" (Jung), 123 n. 69
Reflection, 101, 113; & anima, 113, 121 n. 36; & Athena, 113; as instinct, 101; & masculine, 113; & psyche, 102; as Shakti, 100
The Religions of the Greeks and Romans (Kerenyi), 89

Repression, 33, 34, 70, 80; in fairytales, 86; soul &, 79
Re-Visioning Psychology (Hillman), 43, 55 n. 16, 71 n. 1, 89 n. 2
Rhea, 32

The Sacred and the Profane (Eliade), 123 n. 68
St. Ambrose, 52
Sahasrara 120 n. 29
S'akti & S'akta (Woodroffe), 119 n. 25
Salt, 15
Satapatha Brahmana, 66
Saturn/Kronos, 19, 32, 36, 38, 46, 47, 48, 50, 54; of angelic purity, 52; archetype of history, 32; blindness of, 49; & compulsions, 49; & consciousness, 36, 37, 52; & counselling, 31; as dark purger, 52; & ego, 34; emasculated father, 32; & feminine, 49; inward and outward, 40; as lead, 29; as liberator, 47; limitation of, 51
Schizophrenia, & complexes as partial personlities, 42
Scott, Walter, 56 n. 23
lities, 42
Scott, Walter, 56 n. 23
The Secrets of Alchemy (Paracelsus), 55 n. 14
The Secret of the Golden Flower (Wilhelm/Jung), 27 n. 4, 55 n. 56
Sefiroth/Sefirothic, 60, 105, 110
Self, & ego, 103, 112; God image, 63; & unconscious, 63, 106
Serpent, 70; Alexander the Great as, 115; Asklepios as, 115; & Athena, 115; Augustus as, 115; as consciousness, 64; & Eve, 61; of Genesis, 59, 69, 115; as instinct, 65, 68; as Kundalini, 106; & Kundalini Yoga, 64; as masculine, 115; as Shakti, 100, 115; subtle, 64; & sympathetic nervous system, 64
The Serpent Power (Woodroffe), 119 n. 27, 121 n. 30 & 33
Sexual Symbolism: A History of Phallic Worship (Knight/Wright), 124 n. 79
Shakti, 75, 100, 101, 107, 120 n. 29; created thirty-six worlds, 100; feminine & yin, 95; Maya-, 101; as mirror, 77, 100; as serpent, 100, 115
Sheehan, Prof. Donald, 50
Shekhinah, 75, 104, 105; as Earth, 76; in exile, 75; as fourth Kabbalistic world, 76; as Malkuth, 76; without soul, 76; as unconscious, 105
Shiva, 101, 113, 114, 115; alone, 77; aspect of consciousness, 111; located in head, 103; masculine and yang, 95; as Parashiva, 100; & serpent, 115
Simon, 104
Sin, consciousness as, 61; of Genesis, 59
Skeleton, as feminine, 63; as *mana* object, 63
Sky, as male and Great Father, 33; as Uranos, 37
Socrates, 16
Sol, 78; as consciousness, 35
Song of Solomon, 84
Sophia, 104
Soul, 7, 16, 17, 20, 21, 25, 26, 39, 43, 47, 54, 74, 79, 80, 83, 84, 96, 97, 98, 111; alchemy, product of 18; & anima/animus, 94; Aphroditic trials of, 51; archaic, 58; archetypes not property of, 39; base of, 53; & *bios* & *zoe*, 58; and body, 15, 22, 80; cosmic, 100; of a culture, 24; & death, 48, 53; defined, 43; & desert, 63; of elements, 15; & the erotic, 50; Eve as, 63; in exile, 63, 87; as feminine, 63, 81; function of, 63; heaven of, 52; image of, 48, 75; & the imaginal, 49; & imagination, 26; incurable, 53; inquisitiveness of, 63; Kabbalistic triad of, 76; & Kether, 76; language of, 18; & loving, 50; mediates, 63; Metis as aspect of, 52; as middleground, 43; night of, 52; organs express, 26; personifying tendency of, 36; projection of, 75; as reflective ground, 46; refusal of, 81; rejected, 79; repressed, 79; Shekhinah without, 76; -making, 62; -work, 75; become spirit, 48; stable, 53; & Tifereth, 76; & transformation, 81; of the universe, 66; & underworld, 53; from water, 48; & women, 94, 95; world-, 39; world- as zodiacal figure, 40
Soul, World, see Anima mundi
Spine, 100, 120 n. 29
Spinoza, 17
Spirit(s), 7, 17, 19, 21, 25, 84; & body, 22; breakdowns of, 78; evil, 76; masculine, 81; in Nature, 64; & Saturn, 37
Spiritual Disciplines, 121 n. 31
Spiritualization, 37, 47, 48, 49, 54; & Kronos, 51
Stars, see Astrology
Stein, Murray, 36, 55 n. 11
Suffering, in becoming conscious, 70; & disunity, 70; & transformation, 24
Sulpher-Mercury theory, 15; body composed of, 15
Sun, -channel, 100; Parashiva as, 100
Super-ego, born of guilt, 36
Susumna, 109, 120 n. 29
Svadhishthana 106, 120 n. 29, 122 n. 49
Symbol, 35, 82, 83; visible sign, 82
synchronicity, 23, 24, 96, 118 n. 14
Syphilis, 12

T'ai Chi, 93; & hermaphrodite, 61
Tantra, 100, 110
Tao, of heaven and earth, 119 n. 20
Tartoros, described, 52ff
Tattvas, created by Shakti, 100
Thanatos, 108
Theatrum Chemicum Britannicum (Ashmole), 41
Theogony (Hesiod), 32
"The Theory of the Instincts" (Freud), 122 n. 59
Thompson, Clara, 122 n. 59
Tifereth, & soul, 76
Titans, 32
"Toward an Archetypal Imagination," (Casey), 55 n. 21
Transformation, 43, 64, 65, 70, 81, 82, 83, 85, 91; archetypal process of, 110; & feminine, 81 105; of hermaphroditic natures, 95; of images, 44; & imagination, 58; & Kundalini, 64; of nature, 45; & serpent, 64; & suffering, 24; three-fold process of, 100, 109; wounded god and, 23
Tree of Knowledge, 59, 61, 64, 65
Tree of Life, Sefirothic, 75
Tria prima, 15
Tripp, Edward, 124 n. 84
Two Essays on Analytical Psychology (Jung), 55 n. 17

Ulysses, 97

Upanishads, Yoga, 101
Unconscious, 33, 36, 42, 50, 67, 74, 80, 83, 122 n. 53; as chakra, 105; collective-, 95; & complexes, 41, 42; as feminine, 103; God's, 67, 68, 70; & genitals, 106; as hermaphrodite, 60, 61; & Hermes, 114; inexhaustible, 35; Luna as, 35; in men, 33; as Mercurius, 95; myth of, 107; & opposites, 64; & Paradise, 62, 63; as petrifying, 113; & Self, 63; separation from, 63; & Shekhina, 105; short-cut to, 44; & soul, 63; self, 106; in women, 33; as the world, 70
Uranos, 32, 36, 37, 46; compulsion of, 51; & matter, 37

The Varieties of Religious Experience (James), 118 n. 18
Virgin Mary, 75, 84; & Aphrodite, 49
Vishnu, 113, 114
Visuddha, 120 n. 29
von Franz, Maria 117
von Hohneheim, Philippus Aureolus Theophrastus Bombastus, 11

Waite, Arthur Edward, 27 n. 2 & 6
Water, death to souls, 48; from earth, 48; metallic, 89
Wholeness, 82; archetypal, 43, 47; astrological, 41, 43; & dark night of the soul, 52; life as, 23
Wilhelm, Richard, 27 n. 4, 56 n. 24, 119 n. 20
Woman, 74, 77, 86; disregard of, 75; theory of, 74
Woodroffe, Sir John, 119 n. 25-27, 120 n. 28
World(s), as feminine, 76; four of Kabbalism, 104; fourteen of Kundalini yoga, 100; & imagination, 101; -parents, 92; as Shakti, 77; as Shekhinah, 76; thirty-six created by Shakti, 100; three, 76; transparent part of, 82
Wound/wounding, 12, 22; & accident, 24; as archetypal moment, 24; & Christ, 23; exiles us, 24; gods come to us through, 22; image of, 21; love-, 50; & soul, 24; soul message, 23
Wright, Thomas, 124 n. 79

Yang, 88; & hermaphrodite, 61; light & positive, 76; masculine & Shiva, 95; & sexuality, 77
Yesod, 106; & soul, 76
Yin, 75, 88; dark & negative, 76; feminine & Shakti, 95; & hermaphrodite, 61; & sexuality, 77
Yoga, alchemical, 88; & imagination, 101; Kundalini-, 95, 101, 109, 110, 111, 113; Tantric, 61
The Yoga Upanishad (Ayyangar), 121 n. 31
Yoni, 120 n. 29

Zeus, 32, 38, 52, 112, 113, 115
Zimmer, Heinrich, 120 n. 29, 121 n. 31, 123 n. 74
Zodiac, 43; zodiacal archetype & Philsopher's Stone, 41; zodiac & world soul, 40
Zoe, & soul, 58